Fleurs

Bouquets, Arrangements,
and French Floral Inspirations

Fleurs

Adrienne Ryser

Photographs by Katie Donnelly

UNION
SQUARE
& CO.
NEW YORK

Text © 2026 by Adrienne Ryser
Photographs © 2026 by Katie Donnelly unless otherwise credited
Cover © 2026 by Hachette Book Group, Inc.

Hachette Book Group supports the right to free expression and the value of copyright. The purpose of copyright is to encourage writers and artists to produce the creative works that enrich our culture.

The scanning, uploading, and distribution of this book without permission is a theft of the author's intellectual property. If you would like permission to use material from the book (other than for review purposes), please contact permissions@hbgusa.com. Thank you for your support of the author's rights.

Union Square & Co.
Hachette Book Group
1290 Avenue of the Americas, New York, NY 10104
unionsquareandco.com
@unionsqandco

First Edition: April 2026

Union Square & Co. is an imprint of Grand Central Publishing, a division of Hachette Book Group, Inc. The Union Square & Co. name and logo are registered trademarks of Hachette Book Group, Inc.

The publisher is not responsible for websites (or their content) that are not owned by the publisher.

Union Square & Co. books may be purchased in bulk for business, educational, or promotional use. For information, please contact your local bookseller or the Hachette Book Group Special Markets Department at special.markets@hbgusa.com.

Editor: Caitlin Leffel
Designer: Renée Bollier
Photographers: Katie Donnelly, Krystal Kenney (page 36), and Adrienne Ryser (page 191)
Assistant Floral Stylist: Myra Stafford
Production Editor: Ivy McFadden
Production Manager: Kevin Iwano
Copy Editor: Kerry Acker

Library of Congress Control Number: 2025946349

ISBNs: 978-1-4549-5802-4 (hardcover), 978-1-4549-5803-1 (ebook)

Printed in China

1010

10 9 8 7 6 5 4 3 2 1

This book is dedicated to Rose Victoire, who bloomed for a moment and left a lifetime of love.

Contents

9	*Introduction*
13	*The French and Their Flowers*
14	*Traditions and Twists*
18	*Equipment and Tools*
21	*Vases and Vessels*
22	*Creating the French Spiral Bouquet*

L'Arrosoir Ambiance 27

28	**Le Bouquet Signature de L'Arrosoir** *L'Arrosoir Signature Bouquet*
32	**Blanc et Vert** *White and Green*
35	**Plateau de Charcuterie Raffiné** *Curated Charcuterie Board*
39	**Cosmo pour Toujours** *Cosmo Fields Forever*
42	**Soliflor de L'Arrosoir** *Bud Vases of L'Arrosoir*
45	**Bouquet Lumière d'Été** *Summer Light Bouquet*
46	**Bouquet Champêtre** *Wildflower Bouquet*

Romantic Ambiance 49

51	**Bouquet Signature Romantique** *Romantic Signature Bouquet*
53	**Bouquet de Roses d'Espérance** *Hope Roses Bouquet*
58	**La Table du Jardin Enchanté** *Enchanted Garden Table*
61	**Bouquet Coup de Coeur** *Bouquet for Your Crush*
64	**Parfum d'Amour** *Scent of Love*

67	**Être Fleurs Bleues** *Being Blue Flowers Bouquet*
70	**Candélabre Décoratif** *Embellished Candelabra*

Parisian Ambiance 75

77	**Bouquet Signature Parisien** *Parisian Signature Bouquet*
80	**Fleurs pour Anna Wintour** *Flowers for Anna Wintour*
83	**Bouquet Tout Mimosa** *All-Mimosa Bouquet*
84	**Les Fleurs de la Brocante** *Flowers of the Flea Market*
87	**Cheminée Parisienne** *Parisienne Mantle Arrangement*
91	**Bouquet Fleurettes** *Small Flowers Bouquet*
92	**Petits Centres de Table** *Petite Table Centerpieces*

Impressionist-Inspired Ambiance 97

99	**Bouquet Signature Impressionniste** *Impressionist Signature Bouquet*
104	**Inspiré du Jardin de Renoir** *Renoir's Garden*
107	**Les Fritillaires de Van Gogh** *Van Gogh's Fritillaria*
111	**Le Jardin de Monet** *Monet's Garden*
113	**Bouquet Ballerines en Fleurs** *Ballerinas in Bloom Bouquet*
117	**Nature Morte aux Anémones** *Still Life with Anemones*

Indoor Garden Ambiance 119

- 121 Bouquet Signature du Jardin d'Intérieur
  Indoor Garden Signature Bouquet
- 123 Le Bouquet Sauvage
  Untamed Bouquet
- 126 Petit Jardin d'Interieur
  Little Indoor Garden
- 130 Le Jardin Secret
  The Secret Garden
- 131 Bocaux d'Herbier
  Herbarium Jars
- 135 Bouquet Frais aux Notes d'Agrumes
  Fresh Citrus Bouquet
- 136 Bouquet de Fines Herbes de Cuisine
  Kitchen Herb Bouquet

Minimalist Ambiance 139

- 141 Petit Jardin de Passion
  Small Passion Garden
- 142 Juste Tulipes
  Just Tulips
- 145 Nuances d'Améthyste
  Shades of Amethyst
- 150 Un Bouquet pour Ton Meilleur Ami(e)
  Bouquet for Your BFF
- 151 Rêve de Delphinium
  Delphinium Dream
- 154 Ensemble de Jonquilles
  Daffodil Ensemble
- 157 Style Classique Français
  Classic French Style
- 160 Bouquet de Fritillaires Plein de Fantaisie
  Playful Fritillaria Bouquet

Everlasting Ambiance 163

- 164 Bouquet Signature Éternel
  Everlasting Signature Bouquet
- 169 Préserver les Pétales
  Preserving Petals
- 170 Bocaux Magiques
  Magic Jars
- 173 Couronne à Tout Occasion
  Wreath for All Occasions
- 176 Jardin Éternel
  Eternal Garden
- 179 Boutonnière Séchée
  Dried Boutonniere

Holiday Ambiance 181

- 183 Bouquet de Bonne Année
  Happy New Year Bouquet
- 184 Fleurs pour la Saint-Valentin
  Valentine's Day Flowers
- 187 Table Printanière de l'Équinoxe
  Spring Equinox Table
- 190 Muguet du Premier Mai
  First of May Lily of the Valley
- 194 Bouquet des Fiertés
  Pride Rainbow Bouquet
- 197 Fleurs de la Fête Nationale
  Bastille Day Blooms
- 200 Fleurs de Gratitude
  Thankful Flowers
- 203 Bouquet Festif d'Hiver
  Festive Winter Bouquet

- 207 *La Fin*
- 210 *Glossary of French Floral Terms*
- 213 *Acknowledgments*
- 217 *Index*

We create our bouquets on an old bar salvaged from the brasserie down the street, and the vintage tabac sign marks the spot where customers come to pay.

Introduction

I BELIEVE IN DESTINY. How else would I have arrived in Paris with two suitcases and my cat and eventually found myself the owner of the oldest flower shop in the city?

Growing up in San Diego, I was surrounded by the beauty of nature. My parents worked in the floral industry, and I was immersed in a world of blooms and living beauty from an early age. Despite that, I chose a different path—I decided to become a broadcast journalist. But life has a funny way of nudging you toward where you should be.

In college, I learned how to report news and shoot photojournalism, but an unexpected detour changed everything and altered the course of my life. What was meant to be a summer college trip to Italy and Spain with a friend turned into a stop in the South of France, where we stayed with her grandfather's lifelong friend. On a terrace surrounded by the sweet scent of lavender, their grandson walked through the doors and I met Benjamin, a man whose charm was only matched by his persistence.

His determination paid off, and two years later, I made the best decision of my life and followed him to Paris. Little did I know this choice would lead me back to the world of flowers, and I would soon discover an entirely new way of creating floral arrangements.

For my first year in Paris, I lived in the 11th arrondissement with no work visa, so I spent my days strolling through every flower shop in the city. These shops reminded me of home and bridged the distance between me and my family.

On my first wander down rue Oberkampf, I stumbled upon L'Arrosoir. The one-hundred-year-old flower shop was like an antiques store that nature had slowly overtaken and turned into an enchanted garden in the middle of Paris. It quickly became my favorite flower shop, even though the owner would scold me for touching the blooms. I learned that in France, you don't handle the produce, and you don't touch the flowers.

I saw a *Nous Recrutons* (help wanted) sign in the window one day. Though I had tried to avoid the floral industry because I thought I wanted to be different from my parents, the flowers kept calling me back. I realized then that I had found something extraordinary: a piece of Parisian history where nature and history intertwined in the most captivating way, so I practiced again and again the phrase I hoped would get me hired. "*Bonjour, je m'appelle Adrienne. Je viens de Californie. J'aimerais travailler dans votre magasin de fleurs.*" Despite speaking almost zero French, I got the job.

The moment I got my visa, I began working at L'Arrosoir. As life often does, it brought me back to what I was supposed to do.

For two years, I worked side by side with the owners, learning not only the French technical skills of floristry but also the rich history embedded in the shop's walls. L'Arrosoir was more than a flower shop; it was a living testament to Parisian culture, a legacy I felt honored to be a part of.

Working at the shop, I was introduced to how the French view flowers. Picking up a bouquet of hand-tied flowers is a weekly activity that Parisians include along with their visits to the *boucherie* (butcher shop), *fromagerie* (cheese shop), and *boulangerie* (bakery). Flowers are as essential as meat, cheese, and baguettes. Parisians cherish *joie de vivre*. They move with unhurried grace, strolling through the streets, picking out blooms, and nurturing them with intention.

I also discovered flower varieties I had never seen before and learned the art of foraging, finding beauty in plants I once considered weeds. I began to approach flower arranging with a new, more considered perspective: I no longer just put stems in a vase. Instead, I focused on conveying a mood or a feeling. Hand-tied with raffia, with precisely cut stems, every bouquet conjured a unique ambiance.

I developed the *champêtre* style (see page 46), which evokes images of running through a field of wildflowers with arms spread open, collecting everything touched. Sticks and even weeds find an artistic purpose in my creations.

I learned that each bouquet is a piece of art. Although arrangements can inspire you to recreate

Paris, 1930s. Fleuristes in front of the flower shop at 80 Rue Oberkampf. Once known as À La Riviera, the shop would later become L'Arrosoir.

the exact composition, no two people can ever make the same bouquet. The owners of L'Arrosoir taught me to draw inspiration from the ambiance to create my own masterpiece.

When the proprietors announced their retirement and the shop was up for sale, I knew that L'Arrosoir was my calling. The next day, with a heart full of determination, I walked in and declared that I would buy the shop and preserve its legacy.

I was prepared to be an owner of a flower shop; I had brought with me from childhood the ability to identify every plant and flower I had come across. Watching my father wake up every day and head to the same job for thirty years, driven by a true passion for flowers, taught me that this industry is built on dedication. His quiet commitment showed me that working with flowers isn't just about beauty; it's about showing up, day after day, with consistency. That kind of devotion left a lasting impression on me and shaped how I approach my work in the world of flowers. Owning a flower shop means running a business rooted in living things, so if I step away for too long or lose focus, the blooms can fade, and in some cases, not survive at all.

In 2020, despite a global pandemic, with Ben by my side, I signed the papers. I became the new proud owner of L'Arrosoir, ensuring its place in Parisian history for generations to come. With the keys in my hand, it was the beginning of a new chapter that would ensure this historic gem would continue to bloom, and my life would never be the same.

I filled the shop with fresh flowers on Friday morning, and that night the French government announced a lockdown. I stood out front, passing free flowers to anyone walking by, hoping they wouldn't go to waste. On my walk home, I saw discarded flowers littering the streets and wondered about my future. Did I just make a huge mistake buying this flower shop?

Thankfully, the French value beauty and powerfully connect to and respect nature. By the following month, florists were deemed an essential business along with purveyors of food and wine. The government declared that the French people must have flowers.

Since then, the shop has flourished in ways I never imagined. We've had the honor of working on high-profile projects—from Paris Fashion Week to blockbuster films—delivering flowers to the French president and Anna Wintour and enhancing unforgettable events and glamorous galas. Through these experiences, I've witnessed firsthand how flowers can elevate any occasion, transforming spaces and lives with artistry and elegance and affirming my belief in the beauty of dreams, persistence, and the love flowers bring to the world.

Purchasing L'Arrosoir has allowed me to own a piece of history and create magic daily. I pour my passion into every bouquet I design, and sharing that beauty with others brings me joy. Each bouquet represents a tradition that spans generations, blending the wild with the refined, the past with the present.

I am no longer the girl I was when I arrived in Paris with two suitcases and my cat. France has seeped into me, and I've become a new version of myself. Paris led me back to my roots in the flower industry, and the flowers themselves led to self-discovery. I was meant to marry a Frenchman and have a French baby born just near the Eiffel Tower. I have discovered that I was destined to live among flowers and create the L'Arrosoir way.

You are invited to step into my world at L'Arrosoir, where every arrangement takes a handful of blooms and turns them into something unique. In these pages, I'll guide you through the techniques of French flower arranging, teaching you the rules—and when to break them. You'll learn how to forage, craft hand-tied spiral bouquets, and make flowers an integral part of your days, just as they are for Parisians.

Welcome to the magic of L'Arrosoir.

The French and Their Flowers

The French know a thing or two about the good life. So many of us look to the French as vanguards of taste and style, whether in fashion, art, or cuisine. For the French, flowers are an essential part of daily life, not reserved for special occasions like birthdays or anniversaries. French people consider flowers something to be purchased regularly and kept in the home, to be enjoyed all the time.

At L'Arrosoir, we love catching up with our regulars, who come every week to purchase a fresh bouquet. Our clients habitually buy flowers. Sometimes they come in with their kids and explain that they have been visiting our shop ever since they were kids themselves. It's a generational thing. In Paris, most people live in an apartment with no elevator and only a small kitchen and fridge. People don't drive; they take the metro, and there is no big supermarket to get all your shopping done in one stop. The French take their time, stopping at the fishmonger, picking up some cheese from the *fromagerie*, then swinging by their local florist for a bouquet of flowers.

Working with flowers in France has brought so much into my life. When I first discovered L'Arrosoir, I was in awe of how different it was from all the flower shops I had been to in the United States. For starters, I noticed how the flowers were displayed on tables by color. There was no refrigerator to be found. I had never seen this before. Like a kid in a candy shop, I marveled at how every table evoked a distinctive ambiance.

In all things, the French love their rules. There are strict guidelines for everything, from the proper way of slicing cheese based on its shape to saying *bonjour* any time you enter a store to never leaving a party or celebration before they cut the cake. Flowers are no exception, and the French have some very rigid ideas about flowers, their care, and how they should be arranged. Over the past years I've spent working in and running a flower shop in Paris, I have grown to understand those rules and how to break them, beginning with how I became a florist in Paris.

Traditions and Twists

In France, becoming a butcher, a pâtissier, or even a florist isn't something you can do overnight. It takes years of specialized training to truly master the craft. To earn a proper flower certification in Paris, you must pass a rigorous exam and complete an internship with an experienced florist. By purchasing an already established business, I was able to bypass the traditional path and break the rules. Otherwise, I wouldn't have had the credentials necessary to apply for access to Rungis, the renowned flower market just thirty minutes outside Paris where we source our blooms.

When I began working at L'Arrosoir, I saw how differently the French care for their flowers. Instead of adding bleach to the water like you might find elsewhere, French flower shops change the water and sterilize the vases every day. This daily ritual also allows us to recut the stems with a *couteau* (knife), trimming one to two centimeters to ensure the flowers have a fresh surface to drink from. It's a simple but powerful practice that keeps the blooms looking their best.

One essential, you could even say sacred, rule of French floral arranging is the spiral. Picture an arrangement seen through a clear glass vase with the stems all angled in the same direction around a central axis. In California, we called this the hand-tied bouquet. In France, the bouquet is created so the stems go from right to left when looking at the spiral. As I never had formal training, my stems go from left to right. It is one of the many ways I am constantly breaking the rules. In this book, as long as a spiral is created with the stems, it doesn't matter which way they are facing—just as long as they are all facing in the same direction.

THE L'ARROSOIR WAY

With a flower shop on every Parisian corner, what sets L'Arrosoir apart is the carefully chosen flowers. Some florists in Paris have their flowers delivered, but I like to go and scour the market, finding my favorite blooms of the day and negotiating with the vendors. I am simultaneously composing bouquets in my brain while shopping for flowers, keeping in mind colors, upcoming events, orders, and flowers we might already have in store.

Not all French flower shops are the same. There are a few different types of flower shops in Paris. One kind is *en libre service* (self-service), where the customer selects different varieties of flowers prewrapped in plastic and carries them to the counter. Then, the florist will compose the bouquet for them. Our shop functions differently. When customers walk by, they are already captivated by the fresh blooms spilling out onto the street, which invites them in. Upon entering, they notice that the shop is set up like a museum of flowers. The impact of color is what sets L'Arrosoir apart from other shops. It takes your breath away, and the scent is intoxicating!

We have premade bouquets ready to go out the door, or you can hand-select flowers from vases with a florist, and then we compose the bouquet. (Instead of allowing the customer to handle the flowers, we pluck the flowers from vases or buckets ourselves as the customer makes their selections.)

When composing a bouquet at L'Arrosoir, I first ask the client the occasion for which they're creating the arrangement. From there, we take a stroll around the shop, admiring each table and the particular mood it conjures. With each table offering a different color scheme and ambiance, I'll usually pick a few varieties from the same table that will blend perfectly together for a cohesive look. For example, white flowers are only mixed with green. Blues, purples, and cool tones share another table, while red is paired with subtle shades of beige and burgundy.

Upon my arrival at L'Arrosoir, orange and yellow were practically nonexistent—the previous owners had an aversion to these colors. The one exception was in February, during mimosa season, when an entire table would be dedicated solely to mimosa, as it doesn't mix well with any other flowers.

At L'Arrosoir, we embrace the messy and imperfect. We don't carry every type of flower or every color. We do not cater to the masses. We stay true to the flowers and compositions that represent the brand. Our vibe is more of an indoor, overgrown garden, so I'm not drawn to tropical flowers or tinted stems. Instead, I source French wildflowers at Rungis from a local vendor from Barbizon, a charming village just an hour outside Paris. Because of this curated selection, people come to L'Arrosoir expecting a particular kind of bouquet. I let the flowers inspire the designs and the colors we have in store that day. We love the *champêtre* style at L'Arrosoir. Our bouquets are perfectly imperfect. For over a century, Parisians have come to recognize this signature style, knowing exactly what kind of bouquet they'll find when they step into our shop.

In *Fleurs*, I will teach you how to add Parisian charm to a living room mantle and create a romantic dinner table. I will share everything I've learned about how to compose an arrangement, choose colors that work well together, and create various ambiances using flowers. It is important to remember that these compositions are only ideas to be used as inspiration. Any or all of the ingredients can be changed out for something else. Flowers of the week depend on what we've found at the flower market, or in the woods on a long walk with a pair of *secateurs* (pruning shears).

SELECTING YOUR FLOWERS

Know your flowers' origins if possible. Rungis is the biggest wholesale market in Europe, and I have the luck of going there two or three times per week to select our flowers. Most of the flowers we buy come from France, Holland, or Italy. If you're not picking flowers from your own garden or a meadow somewhere, inquire with a shop owner where the stems you're choosing come from. You may be surprised!

When buying flowers, be sure to communicate with your florist and tell them the occasion for which you are creating a bouquet. Let them help guide you in the right direction.

Consider the setting and the recipient when choosing what to put in your bouquets. For example, don't bring a massive bouquet of lilies to a dinner party—their strong fragrance can overpower the room. For a bedside arrangement, opt for softer-smelling flowers like Yves Piaget roses, lavender, or sweet peas to create a calming atmosphere. On the other hand, you can get more adventurous in spaces like the living room, where you can incorporate bolder, aromatic flowers like coriander blossoms or other fragrant varieties. The key is to match the flowers to the space and the mood you want to create.

THRILL, CHILL, SPILL

I always suggest using three to five ingredients minimum when creating a bouquet for clients at L'Arrosoir. While living in California, I used an expression for gardening succulents: For the design to be complete, we need the thrill, the chill, and the spill. I believe you need those same three elements to create an alluring arrangement of flowers.

- The **thrill**, for example, would be a focal flower, maybe something seasonal, and the star of the show. In the fall, this could be dahlias.

- The **chill** plays a supporting role. These could be smaller types of flowers, like thistles or nigella, accompanying our fall dahlias. These are our accent flowers.

- Last but not least, the **spill**. I like to start and end my bouquet using foliage and other types of *fleurettes* (small flowers) because I think the leaves look great at the end, spilling over, creating a romantic feel. A good example would be *graminées* (grasses) or any type of foliage or branches.

WRAPPING BOUQUETS

Wrapping the flowers is a crucial part of building a bouquet you intend to give as a gift. It is the final flourish. At L'Arrosoir, we use craft paper to wrap the blooms. We carry the classic brown and white and have navy blue, bordeaux, or gray for special occasions. The paper color is carefully selected based on the bouquet's hues, choosing either a contrasting or complementary shade to highlight the flowers in the most beautiful way. The flowers are wrapped, simply and tastefully, and tied with raffia. For the last touch we attach our signature translucent L'Arrosoir card. No plastic used—ever. Most of our customers transport their bouquet on the metro or by bike, so however you plan to travel with yours, remember that it's okay if the flowers arrive at their destination in crinkled paper. The journey of the flowers is part of the beauty. I think that it adds character to the flowers when their *emballage* (wrapping) is slightly torn or weathered.

To wrap a bouquet, start by slightly overlapping two sheets of paper on the table. Lay the flowers diagonally across the center, with the heads pointing toward the top left corner. Then, in one simple motion, use both hands to bring the two outer corners of the paper in toward the center of the bouquet. Gather the paper snugly around the stems—right where the raffia holds the bouquet together—and finish by tying the paper in place with another length of raffia.

Equipment and Tools

"Franglais" is the spoken language of L'Arrosoir. I learned certain materials, plants, and even flower names in French and now cannot recall the words for them in English. *Secateurs* (pruning shears) and *couteau* (flower knife) are words I constantly mix into an otherwise entirely English conversation. "Nina, could you please pass me a couteau and secateurs?" is a phrase often repeated at the shop.

To create a French bouquet, not many materials are required. The essentials are:

- At least three and up to ten flower ingredients (a type or variety of flower stem, foliage, or branch)
- Secateurs (pruning shears): Every home needs a good pair of flower cutters—an absolute essential!
- Couteau (flower knife): A small blade, where one side of the blade remains sharp to cut the stems, and the other side is flat because it's held against the fingers.
- Raffia or twine (I use raffia)
- Vase filled with fresh water: Most bouquets require room-temperature water. Warm water is often needed to help certain flowers open more fully.
- Hammer: For certain flowers, like "Boule de Neige" (snowball flowers), you'll need a hammer to help them open and hydrate properly.
- Branch cutter: For big branches, I use a branch cutter, but snapping the branches works just fine.

Some of the bouquets in this book will require:

- Chicken wire
- Floral foam (Oasis or eco-friendly foam work)
- PVC floral tape
- Craft paper
- Floral frogs: Vintage floral frogs are among my favorite treasures to collect from *brocantes* (flea markets) in Paris. They were popular in nineteenth-century France and are intended to sit in a vase or container and hold flowers in place. This works as an eco-friendly version of floral foam—and it's way cuter! They are a special souvenir to purchase and create a minimal arrangement with, or simply enjoy on a shelf.

NOTE: *When the stems are soft and easily cuttable, I like to use the couteau to trim the stems. When they are too thick or rigid, it is best to use the secateurs. For very thick branches, branch cutters are ideal.*

Vases and Vessels

Vase selection can make or break a bouquet. I have slowly built a trove of vintage vases discovered at flea markets, as well as the ones I inherited from the secret cave at L'Arrosoir. (The secret cave is located under a hidden door at the shop. Inside, you can find all of our out-of-season decorations, and many vases and pots.) Depending on where the flowers will be displayed, I might select an opaque vase, an urn, a pitcher, a glass jar, a small bud vase, a vintage mustard jar from Provence, or even a rusty watering can. Because the spiral stems of the bouquet are part of the beauty, I often gravitate toward a transparent vase. When cutting and creating bouquets for Ben's family in St.-Paul-de Vence in the South of France, I opt for a flowerpot from the garden and fill it up with water as a vase.

I enjoy taking a creative approach when choosing a vessel, often thinking beyond the traditional options, but as a rule the flowers should be at least twice as tall as your vessel. It is important to consider your bouquet when selecting the vase, because not every vase works for any bouquet. First, decide where you will position your flowers so that you can choose accordingly. If the flowers are placed on the dining table, for example, they shouldn't reach above your fist if you were to set your elbow down on the table. This is to ensure that you can see your guests from across the table.

I let the flowers inspire my selection. The vase should be wide enough at the top not to squish, allowing the spiral to breathe inside the vase. This helps the flowers last longer. I always fill my vase with water before placing the bouquet, to avoid damaging any flowers later when adding water to the vase.

Creating the French Spiral Bouquet

Creating a quintessential French bouquet is a simple and beautiful way to infuse a touch of France into your home. Defined by its airy elegance, graceful structure, and natural balance, the French bouquet captures an effortless charm. The spiral technique is a timeless method where each stem is placed at an angle, building a harmonious swirl of blooms. With a mix of seasonal flowers, flowing greenery, and a loose, organic composition, you can create an arrangement that feels like it came straight from L'Arrosoir, undeniably French.

The spiral technique involves placing each flower stem at an angle facing the same direction, creating a clean, radial structure. As the bouquet builds, the stems naturally form a spiral pattern. This method looks clean and gives the bouquet great structure and balance—it can stand on its own when tied properly, usually with raffia, ribbon, or twine, emphasizing a natural style.

PREPARATION

Select your flowers and foliage depending on which ambiance you are trying to create, making sure that the flowers complement each other in terms of color, texture, and size. Place the flowers on a table in front of you, separating them by variety.

We clean every stem before making the bouquet. Pick up each flower and evaluate: Is there a petal that needs to be removed or a stem missing its head? If so, remove it from the selection or snip off any unappealing buds. Cleaning the stems feels like a sacred ritual to me. I love letting the leaves and snipped pieces fall to the floor, forming a flower confetti everywhere! It feels a little naughty yet incredibly freeing. There's something deeply necessary about embracing the mess when working with flowers.

Make sure all the stems have been properly cleaned by stripping off any leaves or foliage that would sit in the vase water—usually the bottom half of the stem. Do this carefully by hand, inspecting each stem one by one. If the stem is sappy or thorny, garden gloves can be used to protect the skin. This step is crucial: leaves left below the water line not only rot quickly, which makes the bouquet spoil faster, but in some cases they can also be mildly toxic.

But sometimes . . . I break the rules and leave a bit of foliage in the water, especially if I know it isn't harmful to the flowers. For example, I love using ivy because it looks beautiful trailing in the water. I'll even use a strand of ivy to tie my bouquet instead of raffia. This is perfectly fine; just be sure to change the water daily to keep it fresh. Room-temperature water usually works best, but if you want the flowers to open up a bit faster, you can use slightly warm water instead. I usually fill the vase slightly more than halfway in each vessel; however, every bouquet is different and calls for different care. For example, if your bouquet includes a *hydra*ngea, "hydra" can remind you to give it plenty of water. Poppies, on the other hand, prefer less, so you would fill the vase just a few inches.

BUILDING THE BOUQUET

Begin by selecting your two focal flowers and crossing their stems to form an "X." Hold the point where the stems intersect with your dominant hand, gripping it firmly between your thumb and fingers. With your other hand, pick up a third stem. Lightly tap it on your shoulder—this acts as a cue to help you remember the correct angle. Then bring the stem forward and place it into the bouquet at that same angle, positioning it to one side of the X.

Each time you add a new stem, repeat the same motion: tap it on your shoulder, hold it at a

CREATING THE FRENCH SPIRAL BOUQUET • 23

consistent angle, and insert it beside the existing stems. This repetition helps create the spiral shape, as all the stems begin to wrap naturally around one another. The flower heads should be slightly tilted outward, helping to shape the overall form of the bouquet.

After adding each stem, gently rotate the bouquet in the same direction—about 90 degrees—before adding the next. Continue this process, alternating between tapping, angling, placing, and rotating. As you go, you'll see the original X transform into a well-balanced spiral.

Maintaining the same angle and rotation direction throughout is essential. This consistency ensures the bouquet forms evenly and looks harmonious from every angle.

SECURING THE BOUQUET

Before tying the bouquet, you can check all sides, gently adjusting any flowers that might need to be pulled up or down to fine-tune the balance. Every flower is essential and should be seen. The spiral shape allows for easy adjustment.

Once you have created your bouquet, secure the flowers by wrapping some raffia a few times around the stems below the blooms, where your hands were holding the stems. Then, tie a knot around the bouquet. This should be tight enough to hold all the stems in place, but not too tight to squeeze the flowers' guts.

Once all flowers have been secured, you can cut the stems to the desired length at an angle using secateurs. This increases surface area so the flowers can drink more water, ensuring a longer life. It's best to leave the stems longer, cut, test the vase, and if necessary, recut shorter. You can always go shorter, but you can't go longer. If the flowers are to be wrapped and offered as a gift, leave the stems long so the recipient can select a vase of their own.

KEEPING YOUR FLOWERS HAPPY

The last critical step of any flower bouquet is changing the water daily. There is no other trick or gimmick that works. Changing the water and sanitizing the vase daily is the only way to keep your flowers happy and thriving for as long as possible. To do this, I create a mixture of warm water, vinegar, and a dash of dish soap. I wet a cloth with the mixture and clean the inside and outside of the vase, then rinse completely. Then, I refill the vase with cool, fresh water.

Once the bouquet has been placed in the vase, adjust your flowers as necessary. Flowers are living things, and they will change over time. Don't be afraid to play and rearrange the bouquet. When refreshing the water daily, pull out any dying flowers, refresh with new ones, or just keep the foliage and flowers that are still thriving. It is so fun to watch your bouquet transform over the next week or so, rather than setting it down somewhere and leaving it be.

Besides bringing nature inside our homes, and brightening our days, flowers are *éphémère*, meaning they last for only a short while. Like time, flowers are fleeting, and I love that a bouquet reminds me to enjoy the present.

Why not place flowers in front of a mirror so you can see them from the front and back? This will allow you to appreciate the flowers from all angles.

Listen to Mort Garson's legendary album *Mother Earth's Plantasia*, composed of electronic symphonies from 1976, among your flowers. Whenever I listen to music, especially *Plantasia*, at L'Arrosoir, the flowers perk up and radiate joy and gratitude!

Repeat daily for the best results and happiest bouquets. *Et voilà!*

L'ARROSOIR AMBIANCE

THE L'ARROSOIR AMBIANCE is *champêtre* and poetic. The first time I entered the flower shop and witnessed the style of bouquets I was seriously impressed. Our bouquets are dramatic and opulent, usually grand in scale and often inspired by art, architecture, and music. We display the bouquets on various tables around the shop, and each one evokes a different emotion. Usually composed of seven to ten ingredients, including branches from the garden and swaying grasses, our compositions are natural and appear effortless. They instantly transport you to a field of luxurious wildflowers.

The key is to add a few stems from each variety at once, which gives the bouquet a natural feel. When creating a L'Arrosoir bouquet, you can't go wrong as long as you use beautiful flowers and follow your heart.

Le Bouquet Signature de L'Arrosoir

L'Arrosoir Signature Bouquet

A L'Arrosoir Signature bouquet blends *champêtre* with timeless beauty. Swirly vine tendrils intertwine with cascading branches and delicate elements, while vibrant round flowers pop against garden snippings and foraged stems. This arrangement features a passion vine, a personal favorite shared with my mother, adding a meaningful touch. Nigella (love-in-a-mist), with its light blue petals, contrasts beautifully with the pink tones. There's something about the way the tall foxglove sways against the more robust blooms that I absolutely love. Blending vine cuttings with market flowers from Rungis captures the essence of untamed beauty, perfectly imperfect.

INGREDIENTS

10 blooming spirea branches (also known as meadowsweet or steeplebush)

3 hydrangeas

7 Coral Charm peonies

5 stems foxglove

10 stems forget-me-nots

10 stems nigella (also known as love-in-a-mist or blue spider flower)

10 stems sweet pea

1 passion vine

1 clematis vine

2 dicentra (also known as bleeding heart)

EQUIPMENT

Tall transparent vase

Raffia

Secateurs

1. Fill the vase halfway with room-temperature water.

2. Remove any leaves from the lower part of the stems.

3. Starting with a base of spirea, begin building a spiral bouquet (see page 22): Hold the first stem in one hand. With the other hand, add a second spirea branch to create an X shape. As you introduce new stems to form your spiral, cross each one diagonally over the previous one and rotate the bouquet slightly in the same direction with every addition.

4. Incorporate a few more branches of spirea to create a loose bouquet. Save some spirea branches to add throughout the bouquet, and at the end.

5. Add structure with hydrangeas, spaced evenly in the bouquet in an imperfect triangle. They add fullness and help balance the bouquet visually and physically.

6. Position the peonies a bit higher than the hydrangeas, letting them float slightly above the greenery. Place them evenly but not too symmetrically, keeping the *champêtre* (country or rustic) feel.

7. Add the foxglove stems to give the bouquet height and a vertical pull. Let a few lean gracefully outward and allow some to peek above the peonies.

8. Incorporate lightness by tucking in nigella throughout the bouquet. They have a delicate, misty texture, filling

gaps and adding whimsical movement. Tuck in the forget-me-nots, scattering them around the bouquet.

9. Gently weave in the sweet peas, letting them dance between the larger blooms. Their ruffled petals and delicate fragrance introduce romance and softness. Let a few trail slightly for movement and a just-picked vibe.

10. Add the passion vine and clematis vine. Let the tendrils drape naturally from the edges or intertwine around the bouquet slightly for an organic, undone finish.

11. Finally, add the dicentra. Their delicate heart-shaped dangling flowers are like a secret detail. Let them peek out gently from the sides or front.

12. Secure the bouquet with raffia, then use the secateurs to trim all stems evenly at an angle so they sit cleanly in the vase. Change the water daily to keep the flowers fresh and vibrant.

Blanc et Vert

White and Green

At L'Arrosoir, green is the best color for complementing white. Although many customers assume that white mixes with any color, we convince them otherwise by combining different textures and shades of white flowers and adding a hint of green foliage. The seasonal branches and ranunculus make this bouquet specific to the winter months. When creating your white winter bouquet, incorporate flower varieties in different sizes that complement each other. This bouquet's *genêt*, or broom flower, takes it to the next level with its fragrance. Photographed through the window of the flower shop on rue Oberkampf, this bouquet is ready to be purchased by someone who can enjoy its blooming branches as the days pass by.

INGREDIENTS

3 blooming prunus branches, such as cherry or plum

7 to 10 stems pittosporum foliage

5 to 7 stems genêt (also known as broom flower)

10 astrantias

10 ranunculus

3 *Clematis vitalba* (also known as old man's beard or traveller's joy)

3 ornithogalum (also known as star of Bethlehem)

5 to 7 stems chasmanthium (also known as woodoats or ornamental grasses)

EQUIPMENT

Branch cutters

Transparent vase

Raffia

Secateurs

1. To prepare the prunus branches, use the branch cutters to cut the stems at an angle. If the buds haven't opened yet, soak them in a bucket of warm water overnight.

2. Fill the vase halfway with room-temperature water.

3. Remove any leaves from the lower part of the stems.

4. Starting with a base of pittosporum, begin building a spiral bouquet (see page 22): Hold the first stem of pittosporum in one hand. With the other hand, add a second pittosporum to create an X shape. This will provide structure and create a soft, lush foundation for the bouquet. As you introduce new stems to form your spiral, cross each one diagonally over the previous one and rotate the bouquet slightly in the same direction with every addition.

5. Add one stem of genêt and spin the bouquet by a quarter. Follow this step with two more stems of genêt.

6. Introduce five astrantias, spacing them evenly around the bouquet and spinning the bouquet in the same direction after each addition to maintain a natural, spiral shape.

Continues

7. Incorporate five stems of ranunculus: First, add two at once, then spin slightly and add three more as a group. Adding a few stems of the same variety at a time creates a more natural look.

8. Add two stems of *Clematis vitalba*. Position them so they extend slightly outside the main body of the bouquet.

9. Add the ornithogalum for a striking, star-shaped pop. Place them toward the outer edges of the bouquet and slightly higher than the other flowers. These will draw the eye and add a unique touch.

10. Add the blooming branches individually, rotating the bouquet in the same direction after each addition. (Branches add height and texture while contributing to the L'Arrosoir ambiance.) Arrange them so they stretch out from the bouquet.

11. Finally, add five stems of chasmanthium. These delicate grasses will bring lightness to the bouquet. Allow them to sway naturally and add movement to the overall composition.

12. Continue adding the remainder of the stems in this order until all the flowers have been incorporated into the bouquet; keep spinning with each addition and adjusting for balance until all the flowers have been added.

13. Secure the bouquet with raffia, then use the secateurs to trim all stems at an even angle so they sit cleanly in the vase. Change the water daily to keep the flowers fresh and vibrant.

Plateau de Charcuterie Raffiné
Curated Charcuterie Board

I love creating charcuterie spreads that feel alive and abundant, whether for a private event, a flower-filled atelier, or simply the joy of gathering. The secret is embracing imperfection—leave carrot tops intact, let tomatoes stay on the vine, and allow grapes to spill from a vintage bowl. The day before Ben and I got married, we hosted a flower shop party with 120 of our closest friends and family. Champagne was flowing as French and American friends came together for the first time at L'Arrosoir. The entire counter was piled high with French baguettes and pastries, while the butcher next door generously supplied endless meats and cheeses!

INGREDIENTS

Variety of cheeses, like Brie, Camembert, goat cheese, cheddar, Manchego, and Havarti

Variety of sliced meats, like cured prosciutto, salami, and ham, and spreadables like pâté and rillettes

Variety of vegetables, such as carrots, tomatoes, and artichokes

Variety of crackers, baguettes, and breadsticks

Sweet elements, like grapes, figs, apple slices, berries, jam, and honey

Savory elements, like olives, cornichons, hummus, and mustard

Edible or nontoxic flowers, like pansies and rose petals

Variety of herbs

Mixed nuts

EQUIPMENT

Neutral-tone craft or butcher paper

Tiered serving stands

Small decorative trays

Spreader knives

Small spoons

Porcelain or ceramic dishes

Cutting board

Ramekins

Candles

Vases

Toothpicks

Small plates

1. Cover the workspace with neutral-tone craft paper or butcher paper. (This helps make cleaning up a breeze, and you can write the food labels directly on the paper for a charming touch.)

2. Arrange the large elements first, such as cheeses, bowls, and ramekins. Press edible flowers into the cheeses.

3. Fold meats in or roll them into loose rosettes around each cheese or ramekin to mimic flowers. (For vegetarians, I like to avoid meat touching other elements.)

4. Place fruits and vegetables around the table, draping them from taller points.

Continues

5. Begin filling in the smaller gaps with sweet and savory accents, herbs, and nuts. Spread these elements in trails to guide the eye naturally across the display, imagining how flowers grow in a garden.

6. Use varying heights by stacking the crackers or placing breadsticks into a vase. Surround the table with vases filled with single stems that match the edible flowers.

7. Light candles to create a warm, inviting glow. *Bon appétit!*

Cosmo pour Toujours

Cosmo Fields Forever

It took me five years to convince my husband to let us get a dog. In France, all dogs born in the same year must have names starting with a specific letter designated by the government. It sounds crazy, but as we've seen, the French love their rules. We landed on the year of the "S," but I couldn't fathom being forced into naming my dog something that started with an S just because France said so. I had come to love the cosmos flower partly because the previous owners of L'Arrosoir lived on a cosmos field and would sometimes harvest and bring the stems for us to play with at the shop. *J'adore* the way they burst open and shine like stars in the sky. I decided to break the rules and name our dog Cosmo.

We were supposed to declare his name to the breeder before picking him up, but we never did because we couldn't pick an S name. We knew we were naming him Cosmo, but we didn't want to admit it in case they reported us to the dog police! (You never know.) When we picked him up, I saw that the breeder named him Star on his little puppy birth certificate. It goes perfectly with Cosmo, my Cosmic Star guy.

INGREDIENTS

7 stems raspberry foliage
10 fuschia peonies
2 large flowering artichokes
5 stems pink delphinium
6 stems nigella pods
6 stems white nigella (also known as love-in-a-mist or blue spider flower)
10 stems coriander flower
10 stems flowering sage
25 stems mixed cosmos

EQUIPMENT

Thick transparent vase
Raffia
Secateurs

1. Begin by stripping the lower leaves from all stems, and group flowers by type on workspace for easy access.

2. Fill the transparent vase with room-temperature water, ready to place the bouquet once it's finished.

3. Begin building the spiral bouquet (see page 22) by holding two raspberry stems angled diagonally creating an X shape. With each flower addition, cross each stem diagonally over the previous one and rotate the bouquet slightly in the same direction.

4. Add focal blooms first in layers, starting with the peonies. Add a few, spin the bouquet slightly, and then add a few more.

5. Add the artichokes toward the center, slightly offset for a natural look. Make sure the artichokes are supported by sturdy peony and raspberry foliage stems.

6. Insert delphiniums, some high and some mid-level, to break symmetry.

Continues

7. Add nigella pods near the edges, mixing with a few open white nigella stems.

8. Continue adding stems one by one at the same angle and direction, rotating the bouquet slightly after each addition.

9. Add coriander flowers and flowering sage to fill the gaps and add fragrance and movement.

10. The final layer is the cosmos; save them for last and use in clusters to create a wild texture. Let some spill over, and some rise high above the rest of the flowers.

11. Fluff the bouquet by gently pulling stems outward for a more natural shape. All flower stems should be angled in the same direction, forming a spiral shape with the stems.

12. Once all stems are placed, use raffia to wrap around the stems twice just above where hands were holding the bouquet. Tie the raffia securely. Use secateurs to trim all stems evenly at an angle and place into the vase of water. Change the water daily to keep the flowers fresh and vibrant.

Soliflor de L'Arrosoir
Bud Vases of L'Arrosoir

The counter at L'Arrosoir was spared from destruction thirty-five years ago. When the shop's previous owners discovered that a brasserie down the street was about to tear it out, they rescued it, giving it new life at L'Arrosoir. The vintage 1930s bar now serves as our bouquet creation station and is considered the heart of the shop. On it you'll find a selection of *soliflors*, or bud vases, for sale. These bud vases can be purchased all together to create a nonobstructive table centerpiece, or bought individually as a sentimental gift to be placed on a side table or shelf. I usually opt for a combination of different bud vases— I like to mix and match. And I often use leftover, even broken, flowers and foliage to fill the vases. Rescued flowers on a rescued bar.

INGREDIENTS

5 to 8 stems foliage, such as fern, ivy, or myrtle

5 dahlias

5 to 8 clematis vines

3 stems celosia (also known as cockscomb)

5 to 8 amaranthus (also known as love-lies bleeding, tassel flower, or velvet flower)

EQUIPMENT

5 bud vases of mixed sizes and shapes

Secateurs

1. Set the bud vases on your table, placing a mix of varying heights and shapes next to one another. (Remember that these bud vases are sisters, not twins, and no two should be identical.) Fill each with room-temperature water.
2. Prepare one bud vase at a time, creating a small bouquet for each.
3. Remove any leaves from the lower part of the stems.
4. Before adding flowers to the bud vases, give their stems a fresh snip evenly at an angle with the secateurs.
5. Start by adding the foliage to each vase as a base.
6. Place the focal flower, dahlia, in each vase at varying heights.
7. Add the clematis vines, allowing them to stand taller than the other flowers.
8. Continue building by adding celosias. To create a more natural L'Arrosoir look, only add celosia to three bud vases.
9. Add one or two amaranthus, setting it lower in the vase.
10. Repeat until all the flowers are used. It's fine if not all the bud vases have the same amount of flowers. If any flowers are left over or broken, I add them to the vases or lay them next to the bud vases. The different heights add dimension and interest to the ensemble. Change the water daily to keep the flowers fresh and vibrant.

Bouquet Lumière d'Été
Summer Light Bouquet

Seasons were something I had to get used to after moving to Paris from California, where it feels like summer all year round. While I love watching the leaves turn bright colors come fall in Paris, it always saddens me when they drop, leaving behind bare branches. But then comes spring and those empty branches begin to bloom, and just a few months later, we're rewarded with summer flowers that make the long winter worth it! This bouquet captures the essence of L'Arrosoir in the summer. A celebration of the return of light in Paris and the return of local farmers to Rungis, bringing with them peonies and wildflowers grown just an hour outside of Paris.

INGREDIENTS

10 stems currant greens
20 Sarah Bernhardt peonies
7 Alexander Fleming peonies
15 stems pink sainfoin

EQUIPMENT

Medium vase
Secateurs
Raffia

1. Remove any leaves from the lower part of the stems.
2. Set everything out by variety on a clear surface.
3. Fill the vase three-quarters full with room-temperature water.
4. Start with one stem currant green and one Sarah Bernhardt peony to create the base of this spiral bouquet.
5. With each flower addition, cross each stem diagonally over the previous one and rotate the bouquet slightly.
6. Begin adding peonies, alternating by color and angling each in the same direction. Vary their heights for a more L'Arrosoir shape.
7. Layer in more currant greens, adding greens every few spins between the peonies.
8. Add pink sainfoin to fill gaps and add a light airy texture to the arrangement. Let a few stems extend beyond the other flowers.
9. Once complete, wrap raffia twice around the stems and tie securely. Use secateurs to trim all of the stems the same length and at an even angle.
10. Place the bouquet into the vase. Change the water daily to keep the flowers fresh and vibrant.

Bouquet Champêtre
Wildflower Bouquet

I can always recognize a L'Arrosoir bouquet *dans les rues de Paris* (in the streets of Paris). Its distinctive look sets it apart from bouquets purchased at other shops in the *quartier* (district). A L'Arrosoir bouquet stands out with its captivating blend of colors, textures, and seasonal blooms, making it impossible to miss. The *graminées* (grasses) sparkle like jewelry for flowers, while the branches reach out and pull you in. To create the aesthetic, I draw inspiration from how I was taught to make a bouquet when I was first hired at the shop. It's all about grabbing multiple stems of the same variety at a time and adding them randomly rather than strategically.

INGREDIENTS

3 tortuosa branches (also known as curly willow), left long

10 to 15 cosmos

10 dahlias

1 bunch switchgrass (about 10 to 15 stems)

5 clematis vines

7 amaranthus (also known as love-lies-bleeding, tassel flower, or velvet flower)

EQUIPMENT

Medium transparent vase

Raffia

Secateurs

1. Fill the vase two-thirds full with room-temperature water.

2. Remove any leaves from the lower part of the stems.

3. Starting with a base of tortuosa, begin building a spiral bouquet (see page 22): Hold the first branch in one hand. With the other hand, add a second tortuosa to create an X shape. Allow the tortuosa to extend naturally beyond the bouquet. As you introduce new stems to form your spiral, cross each one diagonally over the previous one and rotate the bouquet slightly in the same direction with every addition.

4. Add three stems of cosmos and spin the bouquet by a quarter.

5. Incorporate two dahlias and spin. Repeat with three more dahlias on the other side.

6. Add a few stems of switchgrass, then give the bouquet a spin. I love to save some switchgrass for the end, so it sparkles all over the bouquet. Add another switchgrass stem, then add two clematis vines, spinning the bouquet in the same direction after each addition to balance the composition. The spiral shape should now be forming.

7. Incorporate flowers by adding a few sprigs at a time. Add three more cosmos, then two more clematis vines, spinning after every addition. Add the remaining switchgrass, and the last tortuosa.

8. Reserve the amaranthus for the final touches, scattering it throughout the lower part of the bouquet and spinning each time. It creates a natural effect with the amaranthus spilling over, the tortuosa reaching out, and the other blooms nestled in the center. It's the perfect blend of thrill, chill, and spill.

9. Secure the bouquet with raffia, then use the secateurs to trim all stems at an even angle so they sit cleanly in the vase. Change the water daily to keep the flowers fresh and vibrant.

ROMANTIC AMBIANCE

I'VE ALWAYS FELT THAT flowers can sense the energy around them. I often converse with the flowers, complimenting them or asking them to perk up, please. When arranging, let the romance flow through every step, whispering sweet nothings as you gently clean their stems. Creating a romantic ambiance with flowers is like weaving a love story through petals and fragrance. Flowers like lavender, jasmine, and sweet pea not only add visual beauty but also infuse the air with a delicate perfume, adding an extra layer of amour. Together, these elements invite connection, turning an ordinary space into an oasis of romantic allure. Infuse your blooms with love, talk to them while you arrange, play them your favorite French love song, and watch as they come together to cultivate a romantic ambiance.

Bouquet Signature Romantique
Romantic Signature Bouquet

A romantic bouquet is like falling in love. Soft, vintage colors embracing each other like two sweethearts strolling along the Seine at sunset.

When I took over L'Arrosoir, it already had a love story of its own. The previous owners met when it was owned solely by Alain. Christine walked by the shop daily on her way to work. One morning, Alain handed her a bouquet, and that simple gesture turned into a thirty-five-year love and partnership in the shop. L'Arrosoir became part of my love story, too. On Christmas Eve, Benjamin proposed to me right there in the middle of the twinkling store. After I said yes, we jumped into the truck and spent the night delivering Christmas trees to a few last-minute clients across Paris. It was a night to remember.

INGREDIENTS

1 apple blossom branch

15 garden roses

Variegated foliage

10 stems nigella (also known as love-in-a-mist or blue spider flower)

3 dahlias

5 blooming spirea branches (also known as meadowsweet or steeplebush)

7 fritillaria

7 butterfly ranunculus

7 pink peonies

10 stems chasmanthium (also known as woodoats or ornamental grasses)

3 lotus pods

5 stems viburnum

5 pink larkspur

10 stems sweet pea

EQUIPMENT

Branch cutters

Tall transparent vase

Raffia

Secateurs

Craft paper (optional)

1. To prepare the apple blossom branch, use the branch cutters to make a clean cut at an angle. If the buds haven't opened yet, soak the cut ends in a bucket of warm water overnight.
2. Fill the vase three-quarters full with room-temperature water.
3. Remove any leaves from the lower part of the stems.
4. Starting with a base of sturdy stems such as garden roses and variegated foliage, begin building a spiral bouquet (see page 22): Cross each stem over the previous one, forming a loose X shape. As you introduce new stems to form your spiral, cross each one diagonally over the previous one and rotate the bouquet slightly in the same direction with every addition.

Continues

5. Add a few stems at a time, alternating between textures and flower types. Incorporate nigella, give the bouquet a slight spin, then add dahlias, followed by a few branches of spirea.

6. Introduce fritillaria and butterfly ranunculus as airy, dancing elements that bring life and movement to the arrangement.

7. Layer in garden roses and peonies as the focal blooms, spacing them evenly throughout the composition to maintain balance and harmony.

8. Continue by integrating chasmanthium to add a sense of airiness. Lotus pods bring texture and a point of interest, while viburnum adds fullness and structure. Keep rotating the bouquet slowly as you add each new stem, helping to maintain the spiral shape and overall balance.

9. Gently place the larkspur, allowing the stems to rise slightly.

10. Follow with the apple blossom branch, positioning it toward the back and slightly off-center for an asymmetrical, natural touch.

11. Add sweet peas in small clusters, two or three stems at a time, to create fragrant, delicate groupings that visually soften the bouquet.

12. Add any remaining stems to the bouquet.

13. Once the bouquet feels complete, you can make minor adjustments. The grip can be loosened or tightened, and any hidden or crowded flowers can be repositioned. Varying stem heights, some slightly higher, others lower, add to the effortless, natural look.

14. When the desired shape is achieved, secure the bouquet tightly with raffia.

15. Finally, use the secateurs to trim all stems at an even angle so they sit cleanly in the vase. Change the water daily to keep the flowers fresh and vibrant. If gifting the bouquet, wrap the flowers in craft paper and tie with raffia.

Bouquet de Roses d'Espérance

Hope Roses Bouquet

This bouquet was photographed inside a timeworn fountain just beyond the doors of L'Arrosoir. Unlike the grand fountains in Parisian squares, this one is intimate and full of character, a weathered stone fixture nestled in the courtyard of a classic Haussmannian building. L'Arrosoir has stood here for over a century, and I often wonder how many flowers and plants have been lovingly watered with help from this very fountain. She still serves us daily, filling our watering cans, quite poetically—as *l'arrosoir* means "watering can" in French. Delicate layering of textures, scents, and colors takes this bouquet from simple to extraordinary. With each stem thoughtfully placed in a hand-tied spiral, the effect is quintessentially French—and so, so romantic.

INGREDIENTS

10 stems autumnal eucalyptus

3 stems asparagus fern

12 roses (this variety is called "Espérance," translating to "hope")

10 white astrantias

5 tuberoses

10 stems Queen Anne's lace

1 stem snowball viburnum

2 blooming quince branches

1 camellia branch

EQUIPMENT

Tall vase (optional)

Raffia

Secateurs

1. If using a vase, select something tall enough to support the branches. Fill it three-quarters full with room-temperature water.

2. Remove any leaves from the lower part of the stems.

3. To prepare the quince branches, use the branch cutters to cut the stems at an angle. If the buds haven't opened yet, soak them in a bucket of warm water overnight.

4. Begin building a spiral bouquet (see page 22): Hold one eucalyptus stem in one hand. With the other hand, add an asparagus fern to form an X shape, creating a soft, textural base. As you introduce new stems to form your spiral, cross each one diagonally over the previous one and rotate the bouquet slightly in the same direction with every addition.

5. Add two or three roses, holding them at a diagonal and placing them on one side of the X.

6. Continue alternating between roses, eucalyptus, and ferns, and add astrantias for a light texture.

7. Place the tuberoses slightly higher for visual interest. Add the Queen Anne's lace evenly throughout for airiness.

8. Add the snowball viburnum toward the center to nestle in the blooms.

Continues

9. Continue with more roses, spacing them apart so each one has room to open.

10. Carefully place the quince branches and camellia toward the back or slightly off-center for an asymmetrical balance.

11. Fill any gaps in the bouquet with leftover eucalyptus and astrantias, then adjust the stems until the shape looks balanced. Add any remaining flowers or foliage to complete the arrangement and, finally, secure the bouquet with raffia.

12. Use the secateurs to trim all stems at an even angle so the bouquet can sit cleanly in a vase or stand independently. Change the water daily to keep the flowers fresh and vibrant.

La Table du Jardin Enchanté

Enchanted Garden Table

What I love most about creating an enchanted garden centerpiece is that everyone at the table discovers something a little different—something just for them. It might be a tiny bird's nest with freckled eggs, a patch of moss with muscari peeking through, a cluster of mushrooms, or a silver dish filled with fresh herbs. Maybe it's a single cornflower, reaching from a vintage floral frog. Each detail adds a bit of surprise. The key is to have fun, use what is available, and let creativity and imagination run wild. It all comes together to create a romantic, candlelit, secret garden ambiance.

INGREDIENTS

Moss

5 muscari plants (also known as grape hyacinth)

Variety of mini herb plants, such as thyme, rosemary, oregano, and sage

5 mini fern plants

15 to 20 blue cornflowers

5 tall stems sanguisorba (also known as burnet)

Dried mushrooms, mini bird nests, freckled eggs, and other natural elements

EQUIPMENT

5 bud vases

5 to 10 shallow containers, such as glass bowls, silver ice cream bowls, or small dishes

5 to 10 flower frogs

3 to 5 candelabras of differing heights

9 to 15 candlesticks

1. Fill the bud vases two-thirds full with room-temperature water.
2. Set the scene by preparing a natural surface for the tablescape: Use the moss to create a table runner down the center of the table.
3. Remove the dirt from the muscari bulbs to expose their roots. Delicately place them in a shallow container.
4. Gently place each herb plant in a shallow container, allowing the fragrant stems to spill over the edges. Use the moss to wrap around the roots.
5. Distribute the mini fern plants in shallow containers around the table in a balanced yet natural way. Their delicate fronds will evoke a sense of wild beauty, and their greenery will complement the herbs and flowers.
6. Scatter the blue cornflowers in small bud vases or flower frogs throughout the setup. These vibrant flowers add charm and color to the table.
7. Position the sanguisorba stems in the bud vases, bringing height and movement to the table. Use the flower frogs in strategic spots to keep certain stems in place.
8. Introduce dried mushrooms, mini bird nests, freckled eggs, and other natural elements to the display, tucking them into corners or between plants, creating secret little surprises that guests will discover as they move around the table. These organic details add a sense of wonder and discovery.
9. Place the candlesticks in the candelabras, then set them on the table. Let the flickering flames bounce off the plants and create shadows, bringing an element of romance and warmth.

ROMANTIC AMBIANCE • 59

Bouquet Coup de Coeur

Bouquet for Your Crush

This bouquet is ideal for any *coup de foudre*, a French term that translates to "lightning strike" but refers to love at first sight, because receiving flowers can feel just as electrifying as a sudden spark. Every day at L'Arrosoir, at least one customer walks in hoping to craft a unique bouquet for their *amoureuse* (lover). Here's a foolproof arrangement perfect for friends and neighbors—but especially your crush.

INGREDIENTS

5 stems abelia (also known as honeysuckle)
10 stems flowering dill
10 dahlias
1 hydrangea
3 clematis vines
10 phlox

EQUIPMENT

Raffia
Secateurs
Craft paper (optional)

1. Remove any leaves from the lower part of the stems.

2. Starting with a base of abelia stems, begin building a spiral bouquet (see page 22): Hold the first abelia stem in one hand. With the other hand, add a second abelia stem to create an X shape. As you introduce new stems to form your spiral, cross each one diagonally over the previous one and rotate the bouquet slightly in the same direction with every addition.

3. Take two or three flowering dill stems, holding them loosely in one hand, and add them to one side of the X. Spin the bouquet gently, then continue layering the dill around the base, allowing it to radiate outward from the center to add airy texture and movement.

4. Add the dahlias in small clusters, placing one or two stems simultaneously. Dahlias have bold, striking blooms, so place them slightly off-center to create a more natural and organic look. Continue spinning the bouquet and layer the dahlias into the spiral.

5. Hydrangeas, true to their name, need plenty of hydration. Before adding it to this bouquet, gently plunge the flower head into water, giving it a fresh drink. Incorporate the hydrangea, positioning it slightly to the side of the bouquet.

6. Weave the clematis vines into the arrangement, allowing them to spill naturally from the bouquet for a whimsical touch.

7. Finally, place the phlox around the outer edge of the bouquet, filling in any gaps and adding softness and color to the perimeter.

8. Add any remaining stems to the arrangement.

9. Once all the flowers are in place, secure the stems with raffia. Using the secateurs, trim all the stems at an even angle. Wrap the bouquet in craft paper (optional) for a bouquet perfect for any crush.

Parfum d'Amour
Scent of Love

One of my absolute favorite things is when people order online or by phone and choose to include a note with their flowers. It gives me the pleasure of writing the handwritten card and reading the heartfelt messages for the recipient. I've come across the sweetest love notes, and it fills me with so much joy I could burst! This small, intimate bouquet is a gentle gathering of the sweetest-smelling sweet peas and nigella—aptly named love-in-a-mist.

The subtlety of a small, fragrant bouquet adds a sense of *délicatesse* to any occasion whether it's a quiet anniversary, a birthday, or a simple *je t'aime*. Sometimes the right flowers can express what words cannot.

INGREDIENTS

10 to 15 stems sweet pea

10 to 15 stems nigella (also known as love-in-a-mist or blue spider flower)

10 to 15 *Fritillaria uva-vulpis* (also known as fox's grape fritillary)

EQUIPMENT

Small vase with a narrow neck and wider base

Couteau or secateurs

1. Fill the vase three-quarters full with room-temperature water.

2. Remove any leaves from the lower part of the stems.

3. Starting with a base of sweet pea and nigella, begin building a spiral bouquet (see page 22): Hold one sweet pea stem in one hand. With the other hand, add a nigella stem to create an X shape. As you introduce new stems to form your spiral, cross each one diagonally over the previous one and rotate the bouquet slightly in the same direction with every addition.

4. Add one flower at a time, alternating between the sweet peas, nigella, and fritillaria.

5. Keep the shape loose and romantic. Let the fritillaria curl outward, allow the nigella to flutter gently between the blooms, and place the sweet peas so they are consistent throughout. Step back and finesse the bouquet.

6. Using the secateurs, trim the stems at an even angle to an equal length and set the bouquet in a vase with a narrow neck to support the delicate stems. Let the blooms spill slightly over the rim in a relaxed way. Change the water daily to keep the flowers fresh and vibrant.

Être Fleurs Bleues

Being Blue Flowers Bouquet

Born on Valentine's Day, I suppose it was inevitable—I've always been a hopeless romantic. So much so that during my student visa interview, I couldn't help but gush about Ben, telling the immigration officer that I was really moving for love, thrilled to finally live with my French boyfriend. Unsurprisingly, my visa was denied. Years later, in the flower shop, while creating an arrangement that moved me to tears, a client called me *fleurs bleues*. I had never heard the phrase before. In French, it means someone sentimental, a dreamer at heart. She was right—I *am* blue flowers. That phrase stayed with me. So when it came time for our wedding in Montmartre, I filled the museum gardens with every shade of blue bloom I could find—even my wedding bouquet was entirely blue. It was a celebration of love, sentiment, and being blue flowers.

INGREDIENTS

3 cotoneaster branches

5 stems raspberry foliage

5 blue-hued hydrangeas

3 flowering artichokes

3 light blue delphiniums

10 stems purple sage

7 stems blue pied d'alouette, or blue larkspur

5 stems blue thistles

5 stems echinops thistles

5 small blue allium

EQUIPMENT

L'arrosoir (watering can)

Raffia

Secateurs

Branch cutters

1. Fill the watering can about three-quarters full with room-temperature water. Hydrangeas, true to their name, need plenty of hydration. Before adding them to a bouquet, I like to gently plunge their flower heads into water, giving them a fresh drink to keep them happy.

2. Prepare the flowers by removing any foliage from the bottom half of each stem.

3. Place the flowers on a clean surface, separated by variety for easy access.

4. Starting with a base of cotoneaster and raspberry foliage, begin building the spiral bouquet (see page 22): Hold one cotoneaster branch in one hand. With the other hand, add a raspberry foliage stem to create an X shape.

5. Alternate between large focal flowers such as hydrangeas, artichokes, and delphiniums, adding them to one side of the X shape and then slightly turning the bouquet with each flower addition.

6. Add lighter, airier elements such as sage, larkspur, and thistles to the bouquet, allowing them to spill over the edges and fill any gaps.

7. Place another cotoneaster branch slightly outward to create a wild frame; spin, then add small blue allium. Why not tuck an allium into the center of a hydrangea for fun?

8. Let some delphiniums and larkspur stand a bit taller for a bit of whimsy.

Continues

9. Keep turning the bouquet slightly with each addition to help create a full shape.

10. Once all the flowers have been added, wrap the stems tightly with raffia where the bouquet was being held. Tie securely but not too tight.

11. Cut the stems at an angle evenly at the bottom with secateurs or branch cutters so they stand well in the watering can. Make sure to keep them long enough so the flowers sit above the rim, creating a romantic, overgrown look.

12. Add the bouquet to the l'arrosoir (watering can). Change the water daily to keep the flowers fresh and vibrant.

ROMANTIC AMBIANCE • 69

Candélabre Décoratif
Embellished Candelabra

When creating a romantic ambiance at home or in the shop, I love incorporating a vintage candelabra because there's nothing more enchanting than the combination of flowers and candlelight. Whether you're using fresh blooms for a special occasion or dried flowers for a lasting arrangement, an embellished candelabra is unexpected. You can also adapt the same idea to a chandelier or wall-mounted light sconce, which is exactly what we did once while building a mini L'Arrosoir for an exciting Paris Fashion Week event.

INGREDIENTS

- 2 hydrangeas
- 5 dahlias
- 5 zinnias
- 3 thistles
- 3 stems limonium (also known as statice or marsh rosemary)
- 2 tortuosa branches (also known as curly willow)
- 3 amaranthus (also known as love-lies-bleeding, tassel flower, or velvet flower)

EQUIPMENT

- 1 candelabra
- 1 block floral foam
- PVC floral tape
- Secateurs

1. Determine where the candelabra will be placed. If it will be visible from both sides, double the recipe, and add the ingredients to the opposite side of the candelabra as well.

2. Prepare the candelabra by soaking the foam: Place the foam in cool water until it's completely saturated. This usually takes ten to fifteen minutes. Be sure not to force the foam into the water; instead, let it naturally sink to the bottom of the water to ensure proper hydration.

3. Cut the soaked foam into smaller pieces, each approximately two by three inches. Using floral tape, secure each piece to a different arm of the candelabra, wrapping it around twice for extra stability.

4. Using the secateurs, cut the hydrangeas at the stem into four to six smaller pieces, taking the hydrangea from one large flower to a few fleurettes, keeping each stem as long as possible. Hydrangeas need plenty of hydration. Gently plunge the flower heads into water then press these pieces gently into the floral foam. The goal is to use this hydrangea to cover a majority of the foam.

Continues

5. Place the dahlias at varying heights to the right side of the candelabra, using the secateurs to snip each stem before placing it into the foam. On the left side, add the zinnias in an aesthetic triangle shape. I chose to arrange them from dark to light in this composition.

6. Start to fill the empty space and continue covering the foam by adding the thistles and limonium. I love to be very free when adding tortuosa, letting the twists and turns of the branches guide my placement. Save the amaranthus for the end, allowing it to drape down for dramatic effect.

7. Light the candles as the finishing touch. *Et voilà!*

PARISIAN AMBIANCE

CREATING A PARISIAN AMBIANCE is about radiating the same effortless charm that is embodied by the City of Light. It's not necessary to be in Paris or have a collection of French antiques to capture that Parisian magic. Instead, draw inspiration from vintage materials, like weathered vases, aged linens, or patinated pots. Get lost in the melodies of Dalida playing in the background to instantly be transported to L'Arrosoir. The French have a certain savoir faire when it comes to knowing exactly what they want, and I believe the same applies when creating a Parisian ambiance. It's all about tapping into our own inner Parisian.

Bouquet Signature Parisien

Parisian Signature Bouquet

Parisians stop by L'Arrosoir to pick up their weekly bouquet, often on Tuesdays or Fridays. These are the days we receive our fresh flowers from Rungis, filling the shop with the season's finest flowers. The carnation, or *œillet*, as we say in French, is one flower I used to dislike but have now come to adore. I used to think of carnations as a bit passé, but when I started working at L'Arrosoir, I quickly realized how wonderfully fluffy they are, and how they can last for over ten days! Now I can't resist including *œillets* in our weekly Parisian bouquets.

INGREDIENTS

- 1 blooming almond branch
- 10 stems red photinia
- 10 anemones (also known as windflower)
- 10 ranunculus
- 5 stems waxflower
- 7 stems astilbe
- 3 clematis vines
- 3 carnations
- 3 curly allium (also known as ornamental garlic)

EQUIPMENT

- Branch cutters
- Large vase or jar
- Raffia
- Secateurs

1. To prepare the almond branch, use the branch cutters to cut the stem at an angle. If the buds haven't opened yet, place in a bucket of warm water and leave overnight.
2. Fill the vase or jar three-quarters full with room-temperature water.
3. Remove any leaves from the lower part of the flower stems.
4. Begin building a spiral bouquet (see page 22): Hold one stem of red photinia in one hand. With the other hand, add a second photinia stem to form an X shape, creating the foundation of the bouquet. As you introduce new stems to form your spiral, cross each one diagonally over the previous one and rotate the bouquet slightly in the same direction with every addition.
5. Incorporate the larger blooms first, alternating anemones and ranunculus as focal flowers. Arrange them evenly around the spiral, placing each stem at a slight angle.
6. Place the waxflower between the larger blooms. These delicate stems will introduce a light, airy feel to the bouquet and help fill the spaces. Keep these at slightly lower angles, letting them spill around the main flowers.
7. Place the astilbe and clematis vines along the edges of the bouquet to bring movement and wispiness. Allow them to naturally curve outward.
8. Carnations add a pop of color and texture, so place them strategically around the bouquet, balancing out the shape.

Continues

9. Set the allium, with their distinctive round shape, high and off-center, creating a focal point.

10. Blooming almond branches, with their delicate blossoms, bring freshness and texture to the arrangement and can be placed vertically within the bouquet. Positioned at the back or angled slightly, they create a frame that naturally highlights the flowers.

11. When the bouquet has reached the desired shape, gather the stems firmly and secure using raffia.

12. Finish by using the secateurs to trim all stems at an even angle so they sit cleanly in the vase. Change the water daily to keep the flowers fresh and vibrant.

PARISIAN AMBIANCE • 79

Fleurs pour Anna Wintour

Flowers for Anna Wintour

I was honestly speechless when I was asked to create the floral arrangements for an event hosted by Anna Wintour in Paris. She requested poppies and tuberoses, her favorite flowers, so of course we delivered. This bouquet is inspired by that unforgettable evening, when Anna welcomed guests into a classic Parisian apartment filled with the scent of fresh blooms by L'Arrosoir. Iceland poppies are spectacular flowers. Each bloom must be carefully unwrapped by peeling open the fuzzy pod at its base, gently revealing the crinkled petals hidden inside. Once trimmed, the stem ends are quickly sealed with a flame to help them hydrate properly and stay vibrant in the vase.

INGREDIENTS

20 Iceland poppies

5 viburnum

10 tuberoses

1 ivy vine

EQUIPMENT

Tall transparent vase

Secateurs

1. To prepare the Iceland poppies, place them in warm water to encourage them to open. These poppies are hidden inside a hairy green pod. Holding the stem near the head for support, gently peel away the fuzzy shell. Be careful not to rip the flower petals when doing so. Once the pod has been removed, in a few minutes the poppy will fully burst open.

2. Fill the tall transparent vase with cool water one to two inches deep. Although we use warm water to help the poppies open, we use cool water in the vase to help preserve them. (Iceland poppies prefer shallow water.)

3. Remove any leaves from the lower part of the stems, and lay out all the flowers on a clean surface separated by variety.

4. Begin with viburnum as the base for a spiral bouquet (see page 22). Cross the stems to create an X shape, then keep adding stems diagonally, rotating the bouquet slightly with each addition.

5. Add the tuberoses. Their tall form and blissful fragrance bring sophistication and vertical movement to the bouquet. Place them at varying heights within the viburnum base to keep the arrangement airy and dynamic.

6. Bring in the drama now by incorporating the Iceland poppies. Their translucent petals and vivid colors should feel like they are dancing above the bouquet. Use their natural curves to create motion and depth.

7. Once the bouquet is shaped and balanced, wrap the ivy vine around the gathered stems. Tuck the end in securely or tie a gentle knot.

8. Using the secateurs, trim all stems at an even angle so they sit cleanly in the vase. Singe the poppies with a flame; this is known as cauterizing. Sealing the poppies locks in their moisture, which helps them last longer. Place the bouquet in the vase, allowing the ivy-wrapped stems to remain visible—a nod to structure and transparency feels editorial. Very Anna! Change the water daily to keep the flowers fresh and vibrant.

Bouquet Tout Mimosa

All-Mimosa Bouquet

In February, when Paris is dark and gray, a feathery yellow explosion called mimosa brings the joy we need to get through the winter. Ours grows in the South of France, near Saint-Tropez, and I beam from ear to ear when I see the first bundle arrive at Rungis. The fragrance of the mimosa is sweet and delightful, filling the air whenever we line the store's façade with it in abundance. During mimosa season, one can see it all over Paris, displayed in cafés, markets, and boutiques around the city.

INGREDIENTS

3 bunches mimosa (about 15 stems)

EQUIPMENT

Vase

Raffia

Secateurs

1. Fill the vase halfway with warm water, which helps the mimosas hydrate more easily and makes the yellow flowers burst open completely.
2. Remove any leaves from the lower part of the stems.
3. Begin building a spiral bouquet (see page 22): Hold the first stem in one hand. With the other hand, add another mimosa to create the base X shape.
4. Continue adding the mimosa at an angle, crossing each one diagonally over the previous one and rotating the bouquet slightly with each addition.
5. After incorporating all of the mimosa, secure firmly with a piece of raffia.
6. Using the secateurs, trim the stems at an even angle and place the bouquet in the vase. Mimosa only lasts a few days before drying out, so enjoy the fragrance while it lasts! Change the water daily to keep the flowers fresh and vibrant.

Les Fleurs de la Brocante

Flowers of the Flea Market

What could be more French than combining the allure of vintage tableware with a playful touch, turning a simple soup dish into an unexpected vessel for blooms? It captures the essence of spring in Paris, with the excitement of the *brocantes* returning to the city where treasures are found amid the cobblestone streets. The color palette is a delicate blend of soft pinks, wine shades, and lush greens, with each bloom complementing the next. Whether for a special occasion or a casual gathering, this bouquet elevates the moment, embodying the very spirit of a Parisian ambiance.

INGREDIENTS

- 1 blooming almond branch
- 10 stems stuartiana eucalyptus
- 5 stems waxflower
- 10 ranunculus
- 10 anemones (also known as windflower)
- 7 butterfly ranunculus
- 3 green hellebores (also known as Christmas roses)
- 3 clematis vines

EQUIPMENT

- Branch cutters
- Soup dish or low vessel
- Wire cutters
- Chicken wire
- PVC floral tape
- Secateurs

1. To prepare the almond branch, use the branch cutters to cut the branch at an angle. If the buds have not opened yet, place the entire branch in a bucket of warm water and leave it overnight.

2. Fill the dish or vessel three-quarters full with room-temperature water.

3. Using the wire cutters, cut a square of chicken wire large enough to fill the opening of the vessel. Gently fold the corners under to form a soft, cloudlike shape. The wire should have a top and bottom layer; this creates multiple points of support, helping the stems stay in place and giving the arrangement dimension.

4. Nestle the wire snugly into the vessel and secure with floral tape in an X over the opening to hold it steady.

5. Be sure to remove any leaves from the lower part of the stems, and give each flower a fresh cut with the secateurs before adding it to the arrangement.

6. Begin by placing the eucalyptus stems into the wire base, letting them define the shape of the arrangement. Allow some stems to drape naturally while others arc upward to create movement and volume.

7. Tuck in the waxflower, scattering it throughout. Its tiny blooms soften the framework and bring in a touch of texture.

8. Place the ranunculus and anemones next. Vary the heights and angles, letting some sit low and others rise above the greens. Keep them loosely grouped, like a natural garden.

Continues

9. Add the butterfly ranunculus and hellebores. Their subtle tones add depth and softness.

10. Layer in the clematis vines, encouraging the vines to twist slightly through the arrangement.

11. Finish with the blooming almond branch, letting it extend beyond the rest of the flowers, arching outward or rising elegantly to one side. This brings height, seasonality, and a poetic final gesture.

12. Step back and adjust any stems that feel too heavy or crowded. Let the eye wander naturally across the composition. Change the water daily to keep the flowers fresh and vibrant.

Cheminée Parisienne

Parisian Mantle Arrangement

This mantle arrangement exudes an effortless Parisian *je ne sais quoi* where the flowers appear to grow naturally inside. It makes a bold statement in the living room, becoming a conversation piece that draws the eye of everyone who enters. The floral foam base ensures the arrangement remains intact and hydrated, allowing it to continue evolving and blooming with time. It pairs beautifully with my mirror from the *brocante* on rue des Martyrs and my favorite wall sconces from Brocante de la Bruyère. Whether as a seasonal touch or a festive holiday decoration, this arrangement adds an enchanting moment to any occasion.

INGREDIENTS

- 1 blooming prunus branch, such as cherry or plum
- 2 very tall eucalyptus branches
- 15 stems Queen Anne's lace
- 20 blooming spirea branches (also known as meadowsweet or steeplebush)
- 10 white campanulas (also known as bellflower)
- 10 violet campanulas (also known as bellflower)

EQUIPMENT

- Secateurs
- 1 block floral foam (12 x 9 x 6 inches)
- 1 foam tray (12 x 9 x 6 inches)
- PVC floral tape

1. To prepare the prunus branch, use the secateurs to cut the branch at an angle. If the buds haven't opened yet, soak the cut ends in a bucket of warm water overnight.

2. Soak the block of floral foam in cool water until it is completely saturated. This usually takes ten to fifteen minutes. Be sure not to force the foam into the water; instead, let it naturally sink to the bottom of the water to ensure proper hydration. Once the foam sinks to the bottom, it's usually ready for use. Then, fit the soaked foam into the tray and secure by wrapping the floral tape twice around the foam and tray.

3. Start by removing the leaves from the lower part of the stem, and give all flowers a trim before adding them to the foam. Place the very tall eucalyptus branches into the back of the foam tray, forming the tallest focal point of the arrangement and providing height and structure for the rest of the flowers.

4. Incorporate the Queen Anne's lace, placing these airy stems throughout the arrangement. Position them lower to the base and slightly toward the front of the tray to balance the height of the eucalyptus. The soft white blooms of the Queen Anne's lace will add a vintage feel to the overall design.

5. Arrange the spirea branches strategically to add dimension to the bouquet. Tuck them in around the edges, letting them spill naturally over the sides to create an overgrown look.

6. Add the campanulas, placing them gently around the arrangement, filling any gaps. Set the white

Continues

campanulas on one side of the arrangement and the violet campanulas on the other to create more visual interest. The violet campanulas add a pop of color while maintaining a chic Parisian vibe.

7. Add the prunus branch to the mantle off-center where it stands out.

8. Ensure all flowers are securely placed in the foam, adjusting as needed to fill gaps and perfect the overall composition. Keep the arrangement hydrated by adding water every couple of days, as the flowers will continue to drink water from the foam.

Bouquet Fleurettes
Small Flowers Bouquet

Fleurettes is a French word that literally means "little flowers," and I was instantly inspired by these tiny artichokes I found at Rungis—they looked just like miniature fleurette artichokes. We work most with fleurettes in the summer, when all our favorite small flowers are in season and available from the independent French growers. They set up their weathered, rusty stand, often with a glass of wine in hand and dirt still under their fingernails. These flowers were likely cut that very morning, or the day before at most. When combined all together, these little, often overlooked blooms create something big and full of life.

INGREDIENTS

- 10 sunflowers, a mix of chocolate, bicolored, and white
- 5 small artichokes
- 3 green thistles
- 10 stems white cosmos
- 7 light yellow calendula (also known as pot marigold)
- 7 stems black cornflower
- 5 stems Crème Brûlée Phlox
- 7 stems Queen Anne's lace
- 10 nigella pods
- 5 stems Melilotus (also known as yellow sweet clover)

EQUIPMENT

- Opaque container, like a pot
- Chicken wire
- PVC floral tape
- Couteau
- Secateurs

1. Fill the container three-quarters full with room-temperature water.
2. Scrunch the chicken wire into a loose ball, place it snugly inside the vessel, and secure it by taping an X across the top using floral tape to hold it firmly in place.
3. Snip each stem with a couteau or secateurs before adding it to the pot.
4. To create an impactful arrangement with these dainty flowers, begin by placing the sunflowers—the largest and boldest blooms—throughout the arrangement to establish structure and height.
5. Add the artichokes and green thistles low and toward the center, to anchor the composition with sculptural weight.
6. Layer in the white cosmos, calendula, black cornflower, and phlox next, weaving them between larger elements to create a natural flow and softness.
7. Use Queen Anne's lace, nigella pods, and Melilotus as the finishing touches, letting them trail or extend at the edges for movement and a meadow-like feel. Keep the shape loose and garden-inspired, and don't be afraid of asymmetry—it adds energy and authenticity.
8. Finish by adjusting placement for balance. Change the water daily to keep the flowers fresh and vibrant.

Petits Centres de Table
Petite Table Centerpieces

These petite table centerpieces are perfect for dinner parties, as their odorless flowers won't compete with the aromas of the meal. (Fragrant blooms can sometimes overwhelm spaces like dining tables or bedside, making them better suited to living rooms or bathrooms.) Their small size makes these three compositions ideal to use as compact centerpieces, particularly in Paris, where space is often limited. *Pourquoi pas* (why not) incorporate books or glass cake stands to create height on the table? These centerpieces bring a quintessential Parisian vibe, perfect for any *soirée*!

Any small glass transparent container works well: A small vintage pitcher, a tiny glass bucket, or petite glass vases can be used. Mix and match to create a truly authentic Parisian ambiance.

INGREDIENTS

6 blooming spirea branches (also known as meadowsweet or steeplebush)

7 butterfly ranunculus

12 scabiosa (also known as pincushion flower)

10 *Fritillaria uva-vulpis* (also known as fox's grape fritillary)

3 stems wild gypsophila (also known as baby's breath)

EQUIPMENT

3 small glass containers (see headnote)

Raffia

Secateurs

1. Fill the glass containers three-quarters full with room-temperature water.
2. Remove any leaves from the lower part of the stems.
3. Evenly separate the flowers into three mini groups, ensuring each has a balanced mix. The arrangements do not need to have the same number of stems. The variation allows each bouquet to have its own character and charm.
4. Starting with a base of spirea, begin building a small spiral bouquet (see page 22) for each group.
5. Alternate ranunculus, scabiosa, and fritillaria, keeping the stems angled and rotating the bouquet gently to maintain the spiral shape.
6. Tuck in bits of wild gypsophila throughout to add lightness and texture.
7. Once each bouquet feels complete, secure the stems with raffia and use the secateurs to trim all stems at an even angle so they sit cleanly and low in the vases. For ideal centerpiece height, flowers should reach no higher than a fist held upright with the elbow resting on the table. This ensures that guests can easily see and speak to each other across the table.
8. Place the hand-tied bouquets into the glass containers. The stems should be visible through the glass, enhancing the fresh, Parisian feel of the setting. Change the water daily to keep the flowers fresh and vibrant.

IMPRESSIONIST-INSPIRED AMBIANCE

AN IMPRESSIONIST-INSPIRED FLORAL ARRANGEMENT captures movement, light, and nature, reflecting the fluid, spontaneous style of artists like Monet, Degas, and Van Gogh. At L'Arrosoir, we draw inspiration from these artists, and our walls are adorned with Impressionist paintings. When I married Ben at the Musée de Montmartre, where Renoir once resided, I wanted our flowers to capture the same essence. For an Impressionist-inspired ambiance, the flowers should feel loose and harmonious, like Monet's landscapes, and full of life as if caught in mid-motion, like Degas' dancers. Soft pastels, bold bursts of color, and textured blooms mirror the beauty of a fleeting moment, much like an Impressionist painting.

Bouquet Signature Impressionniste

Impressionist Signature Bouquet

Like an Impressionist painting, this arrangement feels like a French floral masterpiece, full of playful light, airiness, and impactful negative space. Each bloom has room to breathe, dance, and shine. Though the bouquet draws from the still-life tradition, using a floral frog and chicken wire brings movement and spontaneity. Impressionist artists didn't just paint flowers; they painted feelings. This arrangement captures a mood. It's not just beautiful; it's impressionable.

INGREDIENTS

14 daffodils

5 stems pittosporum

3 bare spirea branches (also known as meadowsweet or steeplebush)

5 curly allium (also known as ornamental garlic)

3 stems sandersonia (also known as Chinese lantern)

6 burgundy hellebores (also known as Christmas rose)

6 fritillaria

2 stems witch hazel

6 blue muscari (also known as grape hyacinth)

4 white muscari (also known as grape hyacinth)

EQUIPMENT

Secateurs

Flower frog

Footed compote

Wire cutters

Chicken wire

PVC floral tape

1. To prepare the daffodils, use the secateurs to trim the stems at an even angle, then place them in a container with room-temperature water. Allow them to release their sap for three hours.

2. Place the flower frog at the bottom of the footed compote. Using the wire cutters, cut a square of chicken wire slightly larger than the opening of the compote. Scrunch the wire into a loose, circular form that will fit comfortably inside the vase, then nestle it on top of the frog. Secure it with floral tape across the top, if needed. Fill the compote three-quarters full with room-temperature water.

3. Remove any leaves from the lower part of the stems. Using the secateurs, trim all stems at an angle before adding to the arrangement.

4. Start with the pittosporum and bare spirea branches. Add them to the compote to create an airy base that arcs outward and covers the chicken wire.

5. Keep turning the compote as you work to ensure it's beautiful from all angles.

6. Curly allium brings unexpected curls; space them at different angles and heights for a fun texture.

Continues

7. For a natural look, arrange the daffodils in groups of two or three. Let them shine around the compote, clustering some low and others a bit higher.

8. Add the sandersonia next, letting their unique lantern shapes stand tall beside the other flowers.

9. Insert the burgundy hellebores and fritillaria to add drama and contrasting richness. Tuck the hellebores into the mid to low layer of the compote to create depth.

10. Tuck the witch hazel into the arrangement to fill any gaps.

11. Use blue and white muscari as ground cover and texture fillers near the rim. These should feel natural and sweet, like a field edge. Mix the blue and white for a subtle color contrast. Change the water daily to keep the flowers fresh and vibrant.

Inspiré du Jardin de Renoir

Renoir's Garden

You can often find me wandering the hilltops of Montmartre, with Cosmo at the dog park beneath the Sacré-Coeur, or strolling aimlessly as a true *flâneuse* (wanderer) through the winding streets of Abbesses. I always pop into every flower shop on rue des Martyrs as I make my way home. When Ben proposed, I immediately knew we would marry at one of my most beloved spots in Paris—the Musée de Montmartre. We rented the gardens once graced by Renoir and danced the night away among 120 guests. And of course, L'Arrosoir designed the flowers, making the entire evening even more *magnifique*. This hydrangea arrangement, inspired by the centerpiece of our celebration, is simple yet unforgettable. The beauty of this bouquet is how easy it is to effortlessly add the hydrangeas. Renoir would approve.

INGREDIENTS

15 to 20 hydrangeas

3 cotoneaster branches, or any tall branches

10 amaranthus (also known as love-lies-bleeding, tassel flower, or velvet flower)

EQUIPMENT

Large nontransparent vase or urn

Secateurs

Couteau

1. Choose a large nontransparent vase that complements the size and shape of the bouquet. After purchasing the shop, I found this Medici container (see previous page) in the cave of L'Arrosoir. Fill the vase or urn three-quarters full with room-temperature water.

2. Prepare the flowers by removing the leaves from the lower two-thirds of the stems so the foliage stays above the waterline. Remember, in hydrangea there is the prefix *hydra*, reminding us they need sufficient hydration. Give the hydrangea heads a quick dip in water to hydrate them fully. Lay the flowers out on a clean surface, separated by variety.

3. Give the stems a fresh diagonal cut using the secateurs or couteau before adding the flowers to the vessel.

4. Begin with the hydrangeas. Place them evenly around the vase to create a full, rounded shape. Cross the stems inside the urn to help support each other and create structure.

5. Insert the cotoneaster branches next to add vertical interest and draw the eye upward.

6. Place the amaranthus stems so they flow gracefully out from the hydrangeas. For a little drama, cluster them together.

7. Step back and make any adjustments until the arrangement looks balanced and lush from all sides.

8. Recut the stems and change the water daily to keep the flowers vibrant.

9. Secure the bouquet by tightly wrapping the stems with twine or raffia, making at least two wraps around it.

10. Place the finished bouquet in the vase. Change the water daily to keep the flowers fresh and vibrant.

IMPRESSIONIST-INSPIRED AMBIANCE • 105

Les Fritillaires de Van Gogh

Van Gogh's Fritillaria

When I first saw fritillaria in the Jardin des Plantes in Paris, I was in awe. Twisting and towering stems sprouted from the garden beds. Their little bells looked like a place fairies could reside. I couldn't determine which ones I loved more: the dark purple, bright green, or funky orange. Then I stumbled upon a painting of *Imperial Fritillaries in a Copper Vase* by Vincent van Gogh at the Musée d'Orsay in Paris, and my obsession grew. Now I look forward to purchasing them at Rungis every spring. This bouquet is a nod to Van Gogh, incorporating other spring elements from Parisian gardens, such as magnolia branches and allium stems.

INGREDIENTS

3 blooming magnolia branches

12 fritillaria

5 curly allium (also known as ornamental garlic)

EQUIPMENT

Tall terra-cotta vase, heavy enough to support the magnolia and the heavier fritillaria stems

Raffia

Secateurs

1. Fill the vase three-quarters full with room-temperature water.

2. Remove any leaves from the lower part of the stems. Separate all of the stems by variety on a clean surface.

3. Begin building a spiral bouquet (see page 22): Hold the first magnolia branch in one hand. With the other hand, add a second magnolia branch to create the base X shape. These will serve as the foundation for the spiral bouquet, with their bold, large buds positioned in the center or slightly to the side to create structure and depth. When introducing new stems to form the spiral, cross each one diagonally over the previous one and rotate the bouquet slightly in the same direction with every addition.

4. Begin adding the fritillaria, one by one. With each addition, gently twist it around the magnolia branches, clockwise or counterclockwise—whichever direction feels most natural. This motion will form the soft, fluid spiral that gives the bouquet its sense of movement, much like brushstrokes on a canvas.

5. Introduce the curly allium. These twisty, sculptural blooms will bring dynamic energy to the arrangement. Their unique shape creates a sense of movement, perfect for an Impressionist-inspired piece.

6. Add the remaining magnolia branch to the bouquet, followed by more fritillaria and allium, continuing the spiral effect. Once the bouquet feels balanced and complete, gather the stems and secure them with raffia.

7. Gently adjust any stems to ensure a harmonious, natural flow. Once satisfied with the shape, use the secateurs to trim all stems at an even angle and place the bouquet in the vase. The fritillaria will continue to grow, bending and tangling in fascinating ways. Their captivating scent, which might be mistaken for marijuana, adds another layer of charm to this intriguing arrangement. Change the water daily to keep the flowers fresh and vibrant.

Le Jardin de Monet
Monet's Garden

I first visited Monet's Garden in early October, right in the heart of dahlia season. Ben picked me up from my French class at *La Sorbonne* on a Friday and told me he had a surprise planned for the weekend. Two hours later, we arrived in Giverny, and I truly felt like I'd stepped into a painting. We spent two nights and three days slowly wandering the gardens, walking hand in hand and admiring every single bloom. I had never seen dahlias like that in my life. Since then, I've returned to Monet's Garden many times, but my favorite detail remains the ever-changing bouquet in Claude Monet's kitchen. Always colorful and thoughtfully arranged by one of the gardeners, it greets museum visitors with the same warmth and creativity that defined Monet's Impressionism. If I could create a garden-inspired bouquet for that very table, it would look something like this. I hope he would have loved it.

INGREDIENTS

- 10 blooming spirea branches
- 7 "Many Happy" peonies
- 5 garden roses
- 3 alliums
- 5 campanulas (also known as bellflower)
- 5 stems lavender
- 5 stems purple lilacs
- 3 stems white lilacs
- 1 hydrangea
- 3 stems waxflower
- 5 stems currant greens
- 3 stems viburnum
- 3 stems foxglove
- 3 blue delphiniums
- 5 stems genêt (also known as broom flower)

EQUIPMENT

- Vase
- Raffia
- Secateurs
- Branch cutters

1. Fill the vase three-quarters full with room-temperature water.

2. Begin by preparing the flowers, removing any leaves or small side branches on the lower third of all stems.

3. Begin building a spiral bouquet (see page 22): Starting with two spirea branches, form an X shape and then add a peony to one side of the X. Next, give the bouquet a slight spin and add a stem of garden rose at the same angle.

4. Begin to add stems one by one at the same angle, rotating the bouquet slightly with each addition. Remember, hydrangeas need plenty of hydration so gently plunge the flower heads into water before adding them to the bouquet. Alternate between smaller and larger blooms, adding allium, campanulas, lavender, and lilacs between the hydrangea, waxflower, and peonies.

Continues

5. Keep the bouquet loosely gathered, allowing natural bends and movement in the stems.

6. Add currant greens, spin, and then add some viburnum for softness.

7. Add the foxgloves and delphiniums near the outer edges to create some height.

8. Add the genêt, spin, and add the remaining peonies.

9. Keep adding and spinning until all the flowers have been added to the arrangement.

10. Step back and admire the bouquet; see if anything needs adjustment.

11. Once happy with the shape, tightly wrap raffia twice around the bouquet. Tie securely, and then trim all the stems the same length using the secateurs or branch cutters for thicker stems.

12. Place the bouquet into the vase, making sure no leaves sit below the water line. Change the water daily to keep the flowers fresh and vibrant.

Bouquet Ballerines en Fleurs

Ballerinas in Bloom Bouquet

With nandinas stretched out like ballet slippers, and delicate gerberas mimicking a ballerina's tutu, this arrangement conjures a night of ballet at the Palais Garnier. I chose February to create it as it marks the beginning of magnolia season in Paris, when the city streets and charming parks start to come alive with blooms. February is also one of my favorite times to go to the Palais Garnier and watch a ballet, around my birthday. The light pink contrast against the green door reminds me of the colors Edgar Degas used to portray his beloved ballet dancers. For foliage, I used mimosa foliage called "Clair de Lune," grown in the South of France, but any foliage works here. This floral arrangement captures the soft, flowing beauty of ballet, with a gentle balance of structure and movement—a delicate, graceful Impressionist-inspired ambiance.

INGREDIENTS

2 magnolia branches

1 blooming cherry blossom branch

10 stems mimosa foliage (see headnote)

5 ranunculus

3 "Pasta" gerberas

5 anemones (also known as windflower)

3 stems brunia berry

3 stems nandina

EQUIPMENT

Branch cutters

Raffia

Secateurs

1. If the cherry blossom buds haven't opened yet, soak them in a bucket of warm water overnight.

2. Lay out the flowers according to their variety for easy access while composing the bouquet.

3. Remove any leaves from the lower part of the stems and, using the branch cutters, trim the branches to a workable size.

4. Begin building a spiral bouquet (see page 22): Start with the magnolia branches, placing them in an X shape. Their delicate, curved nature creates a beautifully fluid foundation, much like a ballet dancer's pose. The magnolia's presence will anchor the arrangement, providing height and a sense of structure. As you introduce new stems to form your spiral, cross each one diagonally over the previous one and rotate the bouquet slightly in the same direction with every addition.

5. Gently place the cherry blossom branch alongside the magnolia. Its soft, airy petals will mimic the lightness and gracefulness of a dancer in motion.

6. Layer in the mimosa foliage, gently sweeping the stems around the magnolia and cherry blossom. Mimosa has a soft, feathery quality, which adds movement and texture, almost like the flowing skirts of a dancer's costume. Arrange it to look like it's gently swaying in an imaginary breeze.

Continues

7. Place the ranunculus in the arrangement, starting near the center, spinning the bouquet slightly before incorporating each stem.

8. With a gentle twist of the wrist, add the "Pasta" gerberas in a harmonious trio.

9. Add the anemones, their dark, dramatic centers echoing the elegance of a dancer's perfect pirouette.

10. Place the brunia berry stems near the base of the bouquet, clustering them together to create a subtle grounding element.

11. Add the nandina, allowing it to peek out from the other stems. Then, add any remaining stems to the composition.

12. Once all the flowers and foliage are positioned and balanced, secure the stems with raffia, allowing the arrangement to retain its natural flow. Gently adjust the blooms, guiding them into soft curves, as if they're gracefully dancing with the air. Finally, use the secateurs to trim all stems at an even angle, ensuring the bouquet stands tall and poised.

Nature Morte aux Anémones
Still Life with Anemones

On quiet days off in Paris, I love to visit Musée d'Orsay, one of my favorite places to linger and dream. Located inside an old train station, this museum has an iconic selection of paintings. What I love most about Impressionist art is its embrace of emotion over perfection. Instead of focusing on every detail, painters like Monet, Renoir, and Matisse expressed feelings through light, color, and atmosphere. Many of these artists painted anemones, and it's no wonder why. With their vivid petals and dark centers, they are some of my favorite flowers. I especially adore them in a ceramic pitcher I found at the *brocante*—perfectly imperfect, just like the art that inspires me. A vintage vessel helps capture the Impressionist ambiance, like a scene straight from Monet's atelier.

INGREDIENTS

25 colorful anemones (also known as windflower; use a painterly mix of lavender, deep red, and soft white)

EQUIPMENT

Small vase or ceramic pitcher

Raffia

Couteau

1. Fill the vase or pitcher one-third to halfway with room-temperature water. If you want the blooms to open faster, use slightly warmer water; however, cooler water temperatures extend the life of the flowers.

2. Remove any leaves from the lower part of the stems.

3. Begin building a spiral bouquet (see page 22): Choose the first two stems and cross them at slight angles, creating an X. Hold them loosely between the thumb and fingers.

4. Add each new stem at a diagonal, alternating colors, and rotating the bouquet slightly with each addition. This motion gives the bouquet structure, lightness, and natural movement, like brushstrokes in a painting.

5. Adjust so that some anemones sit slightly higher or lower than others to achieve a layered bouquet. The spiral should feel airy and slightly asymmetrical, reminiscent of Impressionist paintings.

6. Once you are happy with the bouquet, secure it with raffia and use the couteau to evenly trim the stems so it fits in the vase or ceramic pitcher. Change the water daily to keep the flowers fresh and vibrant.

INDOOR GARDEN AMBIANCE

IN ONE OF MY first weeks at L'Arrosoir, the former owner approached me visibly surprised, holding a rusty bucket in one hand and a broken wooden box in the other. "What are these doing *dans la poubelle* (in the trash)?" she asked. I had thrown them out, thinking I was helping tidy up the place. But I was wrong.

The rusty bucket wasn't a discarded object—it was meant to hide a plastic pail and add a vintage garden feel, its patina honed after twenty years of garden life before the bucket was found at a *brocante* and brought to L'Arrosoir. The broken wooden box was used to create dimension in flower displays, placing a vase on top to let the tall stems reach even greater heights.

Where I saw broken, they saw potential. Now I understand how weathered elements bring nature indoors and transform a space into a living garden.

Bouquet Signature du Jardin d'Intérieur

Indoor Garden Signature Bouquet

Paris taught me the art of foraging—the joy of looking at my own windowsill for cuttings, or turning to a garden and nature walks to gather what I can. Sometimes I'll even drive the truck an hour out near Fontainebleau to collect branches, moss, and dried ferns for my arrangements. There's something incredibly creative and grounding about mixing store-bought blooms with found materials. The blend creates a kind of indoor garden magic. Often, you don't realize how striking foraged elements are until you see them nestled among other beautiful flowers. It is in the mix that they truly come alive!

INGREDIENTS

- 7 stems raspberry foliage
- 8 Angel Cheeks peonies
- 3 stems chasmanthium (also known as woodoats or ornamental grasses)
- 1 hydrangea
- 3 stems nigella (also known as love-in-a-mist or blue spider flower)
- 3 stems flowered coriander
- 4 stems black cornflower
- 3 stems light pink nerine
- 3 small blooming wild rose cuttings

EQUIPMENT

- Secateurs
- Flower frog
- Footed compote
- Floral putty
- PVC flower tape

1. Remove any leaves from the lower stems of every flower and foliage so nothing sits below the waterline.
2. Cut stems at an angle using secateurs just before placing them into the arrangement.
3. Secure the flower frog to the bottom of the compote (use floral putty if needed).
4. Secure the compote's rim with flower tape, arranging the strips in a grid design for extra stability.
5. Fill the compote three-quarters full with room-temperature water.
6. Beginning with the seven stems of raspberry foliage, create a base layer by adding at various angles to establish overall shape. Allow some foliage to cascade over and cover as much of the grid as possible.
7. Use the eight Angel Cheeks peonies as your focal flowers and place them into the arrangement by grouping in small clusters of two or three, like they are growing together in a garden. Place unevenly for a more natural look. Let a few face different directions to create depth and interest.
8. Add movement using the chasmanthium grasses next to or around your focal areas to bring soft, arching movement.

Continues

9. Gently plunge the hydrangea flower head into water, then add the hydrangea low in the arrangement, covering the compote and adding a pop of pink. Layering is key to creating a lush indoor garden.

10. Place the nigella between the other stems, letting it peek out a bit.

11. Incorporate flowered coriander as delicate filler flowers—spacing them evenly in between the larger blooms.

12. Place black cornflowers to deepen the palette and contrast the peonies. Group a couple together.

13. Add light pink nerines in between the focal points to add height.

14. Tuck in the three small blooming wild rose cuttings as a fragrant touch. Place them low and near the edges as one of your focal points.

15. Step back and rotate the compote while working to make sure the design looks balanced from all sides. Fill any gaps with any remaining smaller stems. Change the water daily to keep the flowers fresh and vibrant.

Le Bouquet Sauvage
Untamed Bouquet

Something I've come to truly appreciate is working with... weeds. At L'Arrosoir, we embrace the beauty of wildflowers, incorporating different varieties into our bouquets. I feel a burst of excitement when the local vendors return in the spring at Rungis with their selections of what I always considered *mauvaises herbes* (weeds) before moving to Paris. Now whenever I'm out in nature, I see weeds in an entirely new light—and often find myself carrying a pair of secateurs, just in case the urge strikes to snip a few. In French, the word *sauvage* means "wild," and this bouquet is a celebration of the wildflowers that naturally grow here in France.

INGREDIENTS

10 stems flowering dill

10 stems borage

5 green thistles

3 bells of Ireland

10 stems *graminées* (grasses)

10 forget-me-nots

1 small bunch miscellaneous weeds

EQUIPMENT

Medium transparent vase

Raffia

Secateurs

1. Fill the vase halfway with room-temperature water.

2. Remove any leaves and thorns from the lower part of the stems.

3. Starting with a base of dill, begin building a spiral bouquet (see page 22): Hold two stems of dill loosely but firmly in one hand. These will serve as the base of the bouquet.

4. Add the borage by crossing it over the dill, creating the first X shape. The borage will add a soft blue contrast, so arrange the stems evenly throughout, making sure they radiate outward in different directions. As you introduce new stems to form your spiral, cross each one diagonally over the previous one and rotate the bouquet slightly in the same direction with every addition.

5. Place a green thistle into the bouquet, then spin it slightly to the side. Add another green thistle, alternating with more dill and borage. This will give the bouquet texture and depth.

6. Take the bells of Ireland, which will add height and drama, and place them outward, one at a time, spinning the bouquet in the same direction after each addition. Now the spiral is starting to take shape.

7. Place the *graminées* (grasses) throughout the bouquet. Allow the grasses to spill slightly outward, creating a sense of movement and adding natural flow to the arrangement.

8. Add the forget-me-nots, scattering them in small bunches throughout the top, center, and sides of the

Continues

bouquet. Cross them over the other elements, layering them to create depth and visual interest.

9. Finally, sprinkle the miscellaneous weeds throughout the bouquet. Use them sparingly to enhance the arrangement's wild, foraged feel, giving it a natural, untamed look.

10. Secure the bouquet by tying the stems with raffia at the base, then use the secateurs to trim all stems at an even angle so they sit cleanly in the vase. Change the water daily to keep the flowers fresh and vibrant.

Petit Jardin d'Interieur

Little Indoor Garden

The word *pansy* comes from the French *pensée* (thought) because the French believed pansies could make your love think of you. We paired pansies and carnivorous pitcher plants in this small Medici vase purchased at the *brocante* in Paris—a wonderful yin and yang, as carnivorous plants derive most of their nutrients by trapping and devouring bugs. Ivy fruit, little stars that emerge from the vine, were also incorporated, among coral bells foliage snipped from my balcony box. Feel free to experiment with the selection and placement of each element in the vase. The beauty of this arrangement comes from its natural indoor garden ambiance.

INGREDIENTS

10 pansies

3 pitcher plant snippings (also known as monkey cups)

3 strands Hedera ivy vine

3 stems Hedera ivy berries (the berries are midly toxic, so keep them out of reach from animals)

5 to 10 stems miscellaneous garden trimmings, such as coral bells foliage

EQUIPMENT

Small opaque vessel

Wire cutters

Chicken wire

PVC floral tape

Secateurs

1. Fill the vessel two-thirds full with room-temperature water.

2. Using the wire cutters, cut a square of chicken wire slightly larger than the opening of the vessel. Scrunch the chicken wire into a loose, circular form that will fit comfortably inside the vase.

3. Nestle the wire snugly into the vessel and secure with floral tape in an X over the opening. (As you position the flowers, tuck the stems into the chicken wire to keep them in place.)

4. Use the secateurs to trim all stems at an angle. This will help them absorb water more effectively.

5. Place the pansies into the chicken wire. These colorful flowers will provide the focal point of the arrangement. Position them around the edges of the vase, allowing them to spill over gently.

6. Place the pitcher plant snippings strategically near each other to create height and visual interest toward the center of the vessel, angled slightly outward.

7. Place the ivy berries and vine stems in the vase so that they gently drape over the edges of the vessel or climb upward, adding movement and a natural cascading effect to the arrangement.

8. Coral bells foliage adds depth and richness to the composition, balancing out the delicate and bold elements. Tuck the remaining foliage into the vessel, making sure to cover the perimeter of the container. Change the water daily to keep the flowers fresh and vibrant.

Le Jardin Secret
The Secret Garden

The secret to bringing a garden ambiance to life indoors is creating an abundant design reminiscent of the natural beauty found in French gardens, where flowers grow closely together in harmonious patches. The result is not just a bouquet but a breathtaking indoor garden that feels as though it was plucked directly from the Tuileries! These designs are ideal for making a bold visual statement or creating a striking focal point. Remember to choose a cohesive color palette that enhances the natural flow and beauty of the arrangement, like shades of green and white. It's a unique way to bring the charm of the outdoors in, turning any indoor space into a *jardin*.

INGREDIENTS

10 stems viburnum

10 tulips

10 stems delphinium

5 tortuosa branches (also known as curly willow)

EQUIPMENT

Small opaque vessel, such as a pot from the garden

Wire cutters

Chicken wire

PVC floral tape

Secateurs

1. Fill the vessel two-thirds full with room-temperature water.
2. Using the wire cutters, cut a square of chicken wire slightly larger than the opening of the vessel. Scrunch the chicken wire into a loose, circular form that will fit comfortably inside.
3. Nestle the wire snugly into the vessel. This acts as a support for the flowers. Secure with floral tape in an X over the opening. (As you position the flowers, tuck the stems into the chicken wire to keep them in place.)
4. Remove any leaves from the lower part of the stems, then use the secateurs to trim all stems at an even angle.
5. Begin adding the viburnum, inserting the stems close together around the front base of the container, forming a lush foundation.
6. Insert the tulips into the chicken wire, grouped closely, with their heads forming a solid block of color. Position them slightly above the viburnum.
7. Add the delphiniums, inserting them in clusters toward the back of the arrangement. The delphinium stems should be tightly grouped together to create a mass of blooms.
8. Finish with the twisted tortuosa branches, strategically placing them to bring movement to the arrangement. Change the water daily to keep the flowers fresh and vibrant.

Bocaux d'Herbier
Herbarium Jars

The Foire de Chatou is a famous semiannual art and antiques fair held just outside Paris. At the fair, over one hundred vendors set out their antique furniture, garden accessories, art, and French collectibles for anyone interested in *brocanting*. People even dress in costume there, and you can, *bien sûr*, enjoy a coupe de champagne and foie gras while shopping. This fair is where I've found some of my beloved vases, including these old medicine or herbarium jars. Just before leaving Chatou, I realized my truck was parked in front of these branches, so I did what I always do: I whipped out my secateurs and snipped a few. I love to play inside my apartment and often move everything around depending on my mood. Filled with butterfly ranunculus, these jars on my dresser feel like I created an indoor vintage garden of my dreams.

INGREDIENTS

3 tall blooming birch tree branches

10 stems eucalyptus stuartiana

10 butterfly ranunculus

2 dried clematis vines

EQUIPMENT

5 jars of differing heights and sizes

Branch cutters

Secateurs

1. Fill the jars three-quarters full with room-temperature water so they are stable enough to hold the branches.
2. Using the branch cutters, cut the birch branches into smaller stems that fit nicely in the jars. Aim for varying lengths to create dimension in each jar. Place the larger pieces in the tallest jars for a stronger focal point.
3. Cut the eucalyptus into shorter lengths if needed using secateurs and place a few sprigs into each jar. The eucalyptus can be positioned in the back and framing the edges, creating a soft backdrop for the flowers.
4. Place two butterfly ranunculus stems in each jar, but trim them so you have a variety of different heights. Make sure the blooms are facing outward and evenly spaced out for a harmonious look.
5. Finally, weave the clematis vines through the arrangement, allowing them to thrill, spill, and chill.
6. Keep adjusting until each jar feels balanced and natural. Some jars may have a taller, more upright arrangement, while others may be more compact and cascading.
7. Arrange the five jars in a row or scatter them around a room to create a cohesive indoor garden ambiance. Change the water daily to keep the flowers fresh and vibrant.

Bouquet Frais aux Notes d'Agrumes

Fresh Citrus Bouquet

Citrus holds a special nostalgia for me, bringing me back to my childhood in California, where the scent of fresh citrus from the orchards would drift through my bedroom window. It also reminds me of my first year working in Paris. The previous owners of L'Arrosoir would clip giant citrus branches from their *jardin* and arrive at the shop with armfuls of them. We'd trim them down and use them in bouquets, tucked between other blooms or as a stand-alone flower. This bouquet includes grevillea, which adds a wild texture and French garden feel. Since citrus stems are thick and tend to cloud the water quickly, I prefer using an opaque vessel like this vintage French confit jar.

INGREDIENTS

7 stems grevillea (also known as spiderflower)

7 fruiting kumquat branches

5 garden roses

5 Julietta roses

5 stems chasmanthium (also known as woodoats or ornamental grasses)

EQUIPMENT

Vase or confit jar

Secateurs

1. Fill the vase three-quarters full with room-temperature water.
2. Remove any leaves from the lower part of the stems, then use the secateurs to trim all stems at an angle.
3. Start by placing the grevillea stems inside the vase to create the overall silhouette of the arrangement. Let some reach outward and upward.
4. Insert the fruiting kumquat branches next. The bright fruit and shiny green leaves provide a captivating scent and original splash of color to the arrangement. Allow the fruit to hang over the vase, like a just-snipped-from-the-orchard vibe.
5. Add the garden and Julietta roses throughout the base and mid-level of the arrangement. Cluster a few together and let others stand on their own to create depth.
6. Finally, tuck in the chasmanthium stems near one side, loosely gathered to create height and a finishing touch of spill. Change the water daily to keep the flowers fresh and vibrant.

Bouquet de Fines Herbes de Cuisine

Kitchen Herb Bouquet

I love incorporating herbs into flower bouquets, or just simply creating an all-herbs bouquet for my kitchen. Any herb can be cut and added to water as long as its stems are long enough. Enjoy them in a vase on the kitchen island, and slowly snip away at their stems to use for cooking purposes. To keep them vibrant and healthy, I recommend adding warm water to the vase every day. This helps the herbs stay hydrated and maintain their aroma for up to a week. The result is a bouquet that delights all the senses. It looks stunning, smells wonderful, and even tastes delicious. *Bon appétit!*

INGREDIENTS

10 stems mint

10 stems rosemary

10 stems flowering coriander

1 tomato vine

EQUIPMENT

Small watering can, or any small vessel

Secateurs

1. Fill the vessel three-quarters full with warm water.
2. Remove any damaged leaves or extra foliage from the lower part of the stems.
3. Lay out the herbs on a table separated by variety.
4. Begin building a spiral bouquet (see page 22) using the rosemary as the base. Create an X shape using two rosemary branches.
5. Turn the bouquet and layer in a few stems of mint and flowering coriander, alternating for fullness and balance.
6. Continue to add more stems of rosemary, mint, and flowering coriander until you have added all the stems and created a spiral shape.
7. Wrap the tomato vine gently, but tight enough to hold all the stems together, around the base of herbs, using it to secure the bouquet instead of raffia. The tomato vine adds a beautiful fragrance and unique flair.
8. Trim the stems of all herbs to a similar length at a diagonal using the secateurs and add to the vase. Enjoy the aroma or snip and use in recipes! Change the water daily to keep the flowers fresh and vibrant.

MINIMALIST AMBIANCE

SOMETIMES, SIMPLER IS BETTER because it allows each element to shine on its own. The French aesthetic embraces this principle where the focus is on subtlety, refinement, and understated beauty. In a minimalist ambiance, every detail serves a purpose, resulting in an arrangement where less (variety) is more (impactful). Each element, whether it's color or texture, is thoughtfully selected to create balance and harmony.

Petit Jardin de Passion
Small Passion Garden

Look at plants for inspiration. Whether by cutting a few flowers in the garden, borrowing a tendril of ivy, or snipping a sprig from a potted plant, a beautiful arrangement can be created with what's on hand. Using natural materials like clematis vine, a terra-cotta pot, and a flower frog, this arrangement brings the outdoors inside, evoking tranquility and simplicity. Ideal for those who appreciate nature-inspired décor, this minimal and whimsical arrangement transforms the simplest elements into a magical little story, adding enchantment to any space.

INGREDIENTS

- 2 peonies
- 2 oat flower sprigs
- 1 clematis vine
- 1 passionflower tendril
- 1 stem dicentra (also known as bleeding heart)

EQUIPMENT

- Small terra-cotta pot
- Flower frog
- Couteau
- Secateurs

1. Place the flower frog inside the terra-cotta pot. The frog will help secure the stems and keep the flowers in place.
2. Using the couteau or secateurs, trim the two peonies to an appropriate length before placing them as the focal flowers. Insert the stems into the flower frog, keeping them spaced slightly apart to allow the blooms to stand tall and prominent. With their full blooms, peonies should be placed at the center or toward the front of the arrangement.
3. Next, insert the two oat flower sprigs around the peonies, allowing them to arch gently over the top or along the sides. The delicate, airy texture of the oat flowers will add a soft contrast to the peonies' fullness.
4. Weave the clematis and passionflower tendrils gently around the arrangement, allowing them to curl and twist. Let the tendrils drape over the sides or rise slightly above the peonies for a whimsical effect.
5. Finally, place the dicentra stem on one side of the composition. Its soft, drooping blooms will add a bit of drama.
6. Step back and evaluate the arrangement, gently adjusting any stems or tendrils to create a natural, balanced composition.
7. Once the arrangement is in place, add room-temperature water to the flower frog, ensuring that the stems are submerged enough to stay hydrated. Change the water daily to keep the flowers fresh and vibrant.

Juste Tulipes
Just Tulips

Tulips have a unique way of moving on their own, stretching and growing toward the light. I once thought tulips were rather dull, but after my time at L'Arrosoir, I eagerly await their arrival each year. This bouquet captures the beauty of simplicity with a single color and variety—no need for mixing. Tulips are most stunning when grouped in one color, creating a clean, minimalist ambiance. They require little water in the vase, but they do drink, so fresh water refills daily help them continue to grow and change. They have a special charm and character, effortlessly bringing life and movement to any space as they reach for the sunlight.

INGREDIENTS

4 bunches tulips (about 40 stems)

EQUIPMENT

Medium vase

Secateurs

Raffia

1. Fill the vase halfway to two-thirds full with room-temperature water.

2. Remove any leaves from the lower part of each stem. Ensure the stems are roughly the same length, leaving them long enough to form a complete spiral and fit comfortably in the vase.

3. Begin building a spiral bouquet (see page 22): Hold the first tulip in one hand. With the other hand, add a second to create the base X shape. As you introduce new stems to form your spiral, cross each one diagonally over the previous one and rotate the bouquet slightly in the same direction with every addition. Each tulip should overlap the previous one just enough to form a natural, loose arrangement. The tulips will naturally lean outward.

4. Continue adding the remaining tulips, rotating and overlapping them as the spiral is formed. Once all stems are in place, tie them together using raffia. Ensure it is tight enough to secure the bouquet, but not so tight that it damages the stems.

5. Using the secateurs, trim the stems at even angle so they sit cleanly in the vase. As the tulips continue to grow in the vase, they will stretch toward the light, adding a dynamic, ever-changing element to the arrangement. Change the water daily to keep the flowers fresh and vibrant.

Nuances d'Améthyste
Shades of Amethyst

What gives this multiflower arrangement a minimalist ambiance is how we use flowers in different hues of the same color. Any color can be selected when creating a monochromatic bouquet, but it is important to utilize varying textures, sizes, and shapes. I created an all-purple arrangement for this bouquet because I was inspired by an amazing lilac vine at the flower market. I had never encountered this particular flower before, and it was the jumping-off point for my all-lilac-tones arrangement. When creating a monochromatic bouquet, let the flowers be your guide to selecting the color.

INGREDIENTS

3 lilacs

10 scabiosa (also known as pincushion flower)

10 anemones (also known as windflower)

5 astrantias

3 clematis vines

7 stems sweet pea

5 stems hardenbergia (also known as lilac vine)

EQUIPMENT

Small vessel

Secateurs

Raffia

1. Fill the vessel three-quarters full with room-temperature water.

2. To prepare the lilacs, use the secateurs to cut the stems evenly at an angle. The bottom inch of the stem can also be smashed with a hammer or split to enhance water absorption.

3. Prepare the flowers by removing all of the leaves from the lower part of their stems and separating them by variety on a clean surface.

4. Starting with a base of lilac, begin building a spiral bouquet (see page 22): Hold the first lilac in one hand. With the other hand, add a second lilac to create the X shape. As you introduce new stems to form your spiral, cross each one diagonally over the previous one and rotate the bouquet slightly in the same direction with every addition.

5. Place three scabiosa toward the center of the bouquet, but at an angle so they contribute to the X shape. These flowers are often used as focal points due to their bold, distinctive petals. Spin the bouquet after each flower addition.

6. Add a few anemones, spin again, and add a few more to the other side.

7. Place a few of the astrantia stems into the spiral, keeping them balanced around the center of the arrangement. This ensures they don't compete with the larger flowers but complement the twisting structure of the bouquet.

8. Place the last lilac stem into the bouquet, making sure it feels balanced among the other flowers.

9. Add the clematis vines between the lilac to create a delicate, airy vibe. Clematis flowers can naturally cascade, enhancing the bouquet's natural look.

Continues

10. Gently place the sweet peas, adding a touch of softness and a delicious scent to the bouquet. Keep spinning the bouquet and adding the remaining flower stems with each turn.

11. Finally, add the hardenbergia to the outside of the arrangement, allowing the foliage to spill over and curve and bend naturally.

12. Once the bouquet is complete and all flowers have been added, secure the stems using raffia and use the secateurs to cut them to the desired length. A French twist bouquet often has an organic, slightly unruly feel so that it won't be perfectly symmetrical or structured, and that is the beauty of it. Change the water daily to keep the flowers fresh and vibrant.

Un Bouquet pour Ton Meilleur Ami(e)

Bouquet for Your BFF

In floral design, "tight" doesn't mean that the flowers are crowded. Instead, it means they are clustered closely together. Layered and dense, this bouquet is as tight as friendship. The flowers are compact and portable, perfect for sharing with a best friend over wine and cheese. When summer arrives and the peonies bloom, this is an ideal arrangement to transport and a thoughtful surprise for your favorite person. It's a bouquet that reflects the closeness and joy of a lifelong (tight) friendship.

INGREDIENTS

10 "Coral Charm" peonies

5 stems rice flower

7 butterfly ranunculus

5 stems columbine

5 stems chasmanthium (also known as woodoats or ornamental grasses)

EQUIPMENT

Raffia

Secateurs

Craft paper

1. Remove any leaves from the lower part of the stems to create a clean base. Each flower should have a nice, long stem for the spiral to hold together.

2. Starting with a base of peonies, begin building a spiral bouquet (see page 22): Hold the first stem in one hand. With the other hand, add a second peony to create the X shape. As you introduce new stems to form your spiral, cross each one diagonally over the previous one and rotate the bouquet slightly in the same direction with every addition.

3. Add the rice flower and the butterfly ranunculus, placing each stem at a slight angle. Alternate between varieties, layering them one by one to create a balanced, natural flow in the arrangement.

4. Layer in the columbines and chasmanthiums, ensuring each flower rests slightly above the one before it. Each addition brings height and flow to the bouquet.

5. Once satisfied with the shape and composition, gather all stems tightly and use raffia to secure them, then trim the stems at an even angle, ensuring they're all the same length for a clean, polished look.

6. Using the craft paper, gently wrap the bouquet to protect the flowers. The paper should be simple and elegant, highlighting the beauty of the flowers without overpowering them. Secure the paper with the raffia. Remind your BFF to recut the stems before adding them to water.

Rêve de Delphinium
Delphinium Dream

Maybe it's because the word *delphinium* means "dolphin" in ancient Greek. Perhaps it's the memory of my sister, mom, and me flying with luggage full of delphiniums for my grandma's wedding. It could be their color, or the way their one stem is made up of hundreds of little flowers, but delphiniums are one of my all-time favorites. This arrangement uses the thrill, chill, spill method (see page 17). In this bouquet, mixed delphiniums represent the thrill, explosion grass is the chill, and spirea branches are the spill. I love how this tapering style of vase hugs the top of the stems, holding the spiral in place, and is wider at the bottom, allowing the stems to stretch out in the vase.

INGREDIENTS

25 stems delphinium, in various shades

10 stems explosion grass

3 spirea branches (also known as meadowsweet or steeplebush)

EQUIPMENT

Tapering clear vase with a wide base and a narrow opening to hug the stems together

Raffia

Secateurs

1. Fill the vase two-thirds full with room-temperature water.

2. Remove any leaves from the lower part of the stems.

3. Begin building a spiral bouquet (see page 22): Hold one delphinium stem in one hand. With the other hand, add a stem of explosion grass to create the base X shape. As you introduce new stems to form your spiral, cross each one diagonally over the previous one and rotate the bouquet slightly in the same direction with every addition.

4. Continue adding the delphiniums at an angle, spinning with each addition. Add a branch of spirea, then explosion grass, then another delphinium.

5. Save a piece of spirea to add at the end, giving extra spill. After all the flower stems have been incorporated, secure firmly with raffia.

6. Using the secateurs, trim the stems at an even angle and place the bouquet into the clear vase to enjoy the gorgeous French spiral! Change the water daily to keep the flowers fresh and vibrant.

Ensemble de Jonquilles
Daffodil Ensemble

The thing about daffodils is they're wonderfully accessible to anyone—blooming in gardens, along roadsides, or popping up in unexpected corners in Paris. That's why I always keep a pair of secateurs nearby, whether in the car or in my bag. I never know when I'll stumble upon a patch of narcissus, and it's fun to gather a few to bring home. Their sunny faces make even the simplest arrangement feel happy, turning something minimal into maximum joy.

INGREDIENTS

Approximately 45 daffodils, of varying shades

5 stems foliage, such as pittosporum (also known as cheesewood, mock orange, or Australian laurel)

EQUIPMENT

A container wide enough to accommodate 45 daffodils and deep enough for the chicken wire (a low, wide bowl or shallow pot works well)

Secateurs

Wire cutters

Chicken wire

PVC floral tape

1. Fill the container halfway with room-temperature water.

2. Remove any leaves from the lower part of each daffodil stem, then use the secateurs to trim the stems at an angle at varying heights.

3. Using the wire cutters, cut a square of chicken wire large enough to fill the opening of the container. Gently scrunch the wire into a loose ball or flat grid shape, depending on the container's size and shape. Nestle the wire snugly into the vessel and secure with floral tape in an X over the opening.

4. Start inserting the daffodils into the chicken wire grid. The wire will act as a natural support, helping to hold the stems in place. Begin with the tallest daffodils in the center, working outward.

5. Group the different daffodil varieties by color or shape for an organized, visually appealing arrangement. For example, group the yellow varieties together, then place the white or orange varieties in their own sections. Tilt some stems so that no flowers block each other. Every flower is important and deserves to shine.

6. Tuck the foliage into the arrangement so it covers the edges of the container and hides any visible tape or chicken wire. Daffodils drink a lot of water, so add water daily and place them in a cool location with indirect sunlight so they can thrive.

Style Classique Français
Classic French Style

At L'Arrosoir, many clients gravitate toward white and green bouquets when gifting flowers to the host of a *soirée*. This palette is timeless and classic and fits into almost any home aesthetic. Photographed in Paris, it becomes instantly recognizable as French not just because of its setting, but because it is minimal, refined, and dense yet full of movement. Compact in size, this arrangement is also practical—easy to carry onto the metro and up five flights of stairs, just like in so many Parisian apartments—without ever sacrificing elegance.

INGREDIENTS

7 stems Cassis foliage

5 to 7 peonies (this variety is called "Bowl of Cream")

10 astrantias

10 cosmos

3 campanulas (also known as bellflower)

5 to 7 stems Orlaya (also known as lace flower)

5 white oxypetalum

5 stems chasmanthium (also known as woodoats or ornamental grasses)

EQUIPMENT

Small transparent vase

Raffia

Secateurs

1. Fill the vase three-quarters full with room-temperature water.

2. Build a spiral bouquet (see page 22): Hold the first stem of Cassis in one hand. With the other hand, add a second Cassis to create the base X shape. This will provide structure and create a soft, lush foundation for the bouquet.

3. Add one peony and spin the bouquet by a quarter. Follow this step with two more stems of peonies.

4. Introduce five astrantias, evenly spaced around the bouquet. Rotate after each one to maintain a natural, spiral shape. Keep the stems tight around each other to evoke a very French style.

5. Incorporate ten stems of cosmos next, adding two at once, then spinning slightly and adding three more all together. Repeat this. Adding a few stems of the same variety at a time creates a more natural look.

6. Add two stems of campanulas. Position them so they extend slightly outside the main body of the bouquet.

7. Add the Orlaya one by one, rotating the bouquet after each addition.

8. Add the stems of oxypetalum for a star-shaped pop. Place them toward the outer edges of the bouquet and slightly higher than the other flowers.

9. Finally, add five stems of chasmanthium or grasses. These delicate grasses will bring lightness to the

Continues

bouquet. Allow them to sway naturally and add movement to the overall composition.

10. Continue adding the remainder of the stems in this order until all the flowers have been added to the bouquet.

11. Secure the bouquet with raffia or choose to let the stems sit freely in the vase, then cut the stems at an even angle using secateurs and add to the vase. Change the water daily to keep the flowers fresh and vibrant.

Bouquet de Fritillaires Plein de Fantaisie

Playful Fritillaria Bouquet

I can't help but do a little dance when fritillaria make their return to the French flower market. These whimsical blooms are so intricate and magical. With just a flower frog, some moss, three stems of fritillaria, and a sprig of ivy, this minimalist arrangement brings me so much *joie*. Whether it becomes a centerpiece on a garden table or sits on a nightstand to bring the outdoors inside, it's a unique and enchanting way to enjoy these dainty flowers. Adding other elements can elevate the flowers, too. An old box or a wooden crate can create height, texture, or just a touch of *je ne sais quoi*.

INGREDIENTS

3 stems fritillaria

Moss

1 ivy vine

EQUIPMENT

Couteau

Flower frog

Small, shallow dish or tray

1. Using the couteau, trim the fritillaria stems at an angle to the desired length, ensuring they are long enough to stand securely in the flower frog.

2. Place the three fritillaria into the flower frog one by one, gently inserting the stems into the frog's holes. Arrange them so they stand tall, like three friends gathered together in conversation.

3. Take a handful of moss and gently pack it around the flower frog, creating a soft, natural base.

4. Wrap the ivy around the moss, winding it delicately and securing it by twisting it around itself, allowing it to flow and curl naturally.

5. Step back and assess the arrangement. Gently adjust the flowers and ivy to ensure balance and that each stem has space to dance. If needed, trim the ivy for a more refined shape.

6. Place the arrangement in a shallow dish of water to help keep the fritillaria hydrated.

EVERLASTING AMBIANCE

CREATING AN EVERLASTING AMBIANCE with flowers is about curating something that you can cherish forever. This can be achieved by incorporating dried or fresh flowers that will dry naturally over time, preserving their beauty long after being cut. For me, dried flowers ignite reminiscence and nostalgia, as most of my dried bouquets or pressed blooms were once fresh flowers for memorable moments in my life. This ambiance captures lasting beauty, much like the timeless spirit of Paris.

Bouquet Signature Éternel
Everlasting Signature Bouquet

Although this bouquet was created with fresh flowers, many of its elements are naturally suited to drying, making it a perfect candidate for a *bouquet éternel* (an everlasting bouquet). The colors may soften, but the bouquet should retain its original spirit and shape. There's no special technique required; just let the water evaporate and allow nature to take care of the rest. I've done this often, especially with bouquets I feel too sentimental to part with. Whether they were gifted by Benjamin or created by me for a special occasion, I can never bring myself to throw them away; I just remove any flowers that have wilted over time. Most people don't realize you can simply let flowers dry right where they are—a beautiful way to preserve a moment and hold onto the memory.

INGREDIENTS

5 stems limonium (also known as statice or marsh rosemary)

5 blue thistles

10 astrantias

5 lavender campanulas (also known as bellflower)

7 stems lisianthus

3 stems lilac

10 stems chasmanthium (also known as woodoats or ornamental grasses)

EQUIPMENT

Medium nontransparent container

Raffia

Secateurs

---

1. Fill the container halfway with room-temperature water to enjoy the bouquet fresh for a few days, then let the bouquet dry naturally for an everlasting arrangement.

2. Remove any leaves from the lower part of the stems, then lay out the flowers according to their variety for easy access while composing the bouquet.

3. Starting with a base of limonium, begin building a spiral bouquet (see page 22): Hold the first stem in one hand. With the other hand, add a second limonium to create an X shape. As you introduce new stems to form your spiral, cross each one diagonally over the previous one and rotate the bouquet slightly in the same direction with every addition.

4. Place the blue thistles around the limonium, letting a few peek out slightly for a more wild, natural look.

5. Layer in the astrantias to begin filling the body of the bouquet. Their star-shaped blooms add complexity without overwhelming the lighter elements.

6. Add the campanula stems to add height and movement to the bouquet with their bell-shaped blooms. Allow them to arc slightly outward to create a garden-grown silhouette. Place them toward the center with the lisianthus and gently layer them in. After adding the lisianthus, place the lilac stems in a loose triangle. Since lilac doesn't dry as well as the other flowers, it can be removed from the arrangement once it begins to wilt.

7. Next, place the chasmanthium into the spiral, angling each new stem slightly with each addition. These elements add movement to the bouquet. Scatter them so that they float around the entire composition.

8. Secure the bouquet tightly with raffia, then use the secateurs to trim all stems at an even angle so the bouquet sits cleanly in the container.

Préserver les Pétales
Preserving Petals

When my mom visits me in Paris, one of our favorite things to do is press flowers in old books. She swears that the flowers hold their color best when pressed between the pages of very old books—there's something about the vintage paper, she says. It's a tradition we cherish every time we're together. We pick a few buds out of my bouquets, remove any leaves that might trap moisture, and simply lay the stem between the pages, distributing the flowers evenly, before closing the book for a few weeks. Once the flowers are completely dry, you can use them in various ways, like framed art, greeting cards, or just as a surprise flower confetti for the next time the book is opened.

INGREDIENTS

Fresh flowers (preferably with thin stems and petals)

EQUIPMENT

Secateurs

Old, heavy book with uncoated pages (hardcover works best)

A flat, stable surface

1. If the flowers have long stems, use the secateurs to trim them.
2. Open the book to the middle pages. Arrange the flowers on the page face down, spreading out the petals to prevent them from overlapping or touching. For best results, avoid overcrowding the pages so that each flower has enough space to dry evenly.
3. Gently close the book, being careful not to disturb the flowers. If the flowers are thicker or larger, place a piece of paper over them before closing the book to keep them in place.
4. To help press the flowers evenly, place something heavy on the book, like another book or a stack of heavy objects. This will apply consistent pressure as the flowers dry, which helps them maintain their shape.
5. Leave the book in a cool, dry place for about two weeks. Be sure to check periodically, but avoid opening the book too often to prevent disturbing the flowers. If they feel dry and crisp, they are ready. If not, leave them in place for longer.
6. Once the flowers are fully dried, remove them carefully from the book for your desired use.

Bocaux Magiques
Magic Jars

Magic jars are an easy way to preserve memories from a favorite event, voyage, or location. You can dry hand-picked flowers in books or use flowers that have air-dried over time. They can be wedding flowers, or flowers picked in the garden on a memorable trip. At my grandma's memorial, we picked flowers from her garden. We preserved lily of the valley and forget-me-nots, along with some of her other favorite flowers, to have something to remember from her celebration of life. They also make thoughtful gifts—I handed out magic jars filled with hand-dried flowers from L'Arrosoir to guests at my wedding. Magic jars are so simple to create yet can hold such significance.

INGREDIENTS

Dried flowers

EQUIPMENT

Secateurs

Small translucent glass vessels (mason jars, small vases, or any transparent jar)

Using the secateurs, cut the dried flowers into smaller bits and remove the stems so they fit nicely in the jar. Then delicately place them inside the jar by hand, one by one, and close the lid. Keep in a dry location out of the sun to ensure the colors don't fade.

Couronne à Tout Occasion
Wreath for All Occasions

Creating a wreath is an opportunity to give life to those dried twigs and flowers that are forgotten at the flower shop. I find that a beautiful wreath is easy to create but greatly impacts a door, table, wall, or even a chair, as it hangs on the back as decoration. What I love about wreaths is that, if stored properly, they can remain everlasting, to be displayed depending on the mood or season. A mix of fresh flowers that will dry over time and already dried stems were used to create this wreath, which adds a unique charm to the everyday.

INGREDIENTS

Grapevine wreath or willow branches

3 fresh ivy vines

2 air-dried hydrangeas

Miscellaneous dried elements, such as various grasses, berries, amaranthus, limonium, and thistles

Dried eucalyptus, lavender, or pine cones (optional)

EQUIPMENT

Wire

Hot glue gun

1. Start with a grapevine wreath. The base should be sturdy enough to hold the weight of the dried flowers but not so thick that it will be hard to work with. If the wreath is too loose or irregular, gently wire, tie, or trim a few pieces.

2. Add the ivy to the base by twisting it around the wreath. Ivy will give the wreath some movement and texture. Tuck the ivy vines into the grapevine wreath and secure them with a dab of hot glue if necessary. Use the glue sparingly so it doesn't overwhelm the natural look.

3. Because hydrangeas are usually large, break them down into smaller florets. Start with a healthy bloom and remove the main stem. Gently spread open the flower to see where the natural groupings are. Carefully pull them apart and separate the clusters. After the hydrangeas are positioned, secure them by tucking their stems into the wreath. Use the glue gun here if necessary to secure the flowers.

4. Start adding the other dried elements (grasses, amaranthus, limonium, thistles, etc.). Work from larger to smaller, filling in around the hydrangeas to create a balanced, natural flow. Bend and twist them to follow the circular shape of the wreath.

5. Once everything is glued into place, step back and look at the wreath from all angles. If any area feels sparse, add a few more dried flowers or ivy to balance it out. Allow the wreath to dry completely.

6. Feel free to personalize by adding other dried elements, such as eucalyptus, lavender, or even pine cones, for a seasonal touch.

7. Keep the wreath away from direct sunlight or humidity, as the dried flowers can become brittle or fade. When storing, hang it to hold its shape.

Jardin Éternel
Eternal Garden

Dried flowers have some advantages. Unlike fresh blooms, they require no water or daily upkeep, yet they can be enjoyed for months, even years, when properly cared for. As sustainable as they are charming, dried arrangements often begin with blooms that were once fresh and already loved. By repurposing these flowers, we extend their story and reduce waste meaningfully and beautifully. Dried flowers carry a nostalgic character and can preserve a moment in time. I often begin with a single arrangement, then gradually add dried stems from other bouquets over time, letting the piece evolve into something layered, sentimental, and entirely unique.

INGREDIENTS

10 stems dried eucalyptus

5 dried hydrangeas

5 stems dried delphinium

1 large dried sweet gum branch

15 stems dried explosion grass

10 stems dried chasmanthium (also known as woodoats or ornamental grasses)

10 miscellaneous dried stems

EQUIPMENT

Raffia

Secateurs

Large nontransparent vase

1. Starting with a base of eucalyptus, begin building a spiral bouquet (see page 22): Hold the first stem in one hand. With the other hand, add a second eucalyptus stem to create the X shape. This foliage provides a loose framework upon which to build. As you introduce new stems to form your spiral, cross each one diagonally over the previous one and rotate the bouquet slightly in the same direction with every addition.

2. Use the hydrangeas to add structure. Nestle them into the eucalyptus. Their round heads will act as the bouquet's visual anchor, so space them evenly throughout.

3. Introduce the delphiniums to bring height and a bit of vertical elegance. Let them dance lightly above the rest of the bouquet, drawing the eye upward.

4. Add the sweet gum branch off-center for height and a touch of woodland texture. It gives the bouquet an asymmetric shape, making it feel like a foraged treasure.

5. Lighten the bouquet by incorporating the explosion grass and chasmanthium. Their sparkling stems will balance the fullness of the hydrangeas. Allow the natural arch of their seed heads to spill slightly over the bouquet.

6. Finish by personalizing with miscellaneous saved stems. These could be anything, such as old strawflower heads, bleached ferns, dried herbs, twigs... Use these special leftovers to fill in any empty spaces and add texture, contrast, and personality. This step makes each bouquet truly one of a kind.

7. Secure the bouquet with raffia, then use the secateurs to trim all stems so they are the same height. Place the bouquet into the container. As long as it's kept dry and out of direct sunlight, the bouquet will last gracefully for years.

EVERLASTING AMBIANCE • 177

Boutonnière Séchée
Dried Boutonniere

My friend Anna once had the idea that we should sell dried boutonnieres at the shop. She used to sit quietly in the corner, tapping away at her laptop while we trimmed stems and welcomed customers. Right there at the counter, surrounded by French blooms, she wrote what would become a *New York Times* bestseller. We began crafting the boutonnieres in those moments, gathering broken bits and forgotten fragments from our dried bouquets. The result was these small, irresistibly vintage . . . unmistakably Parisian boutonnieres. As if they had been dried on the lapel of Ernest Hemingway himself, left there on his smoking jacket from the 1930s—lost in time, only to be rediscovered decades later.

INGREDIENTS

A handful of dried stems like nigella, hydrangea, dried berries, amaranthus, grasses, or Queen Anne's lace

Feathers, vintage brooches, or curly twigs to add a unique touch

EQUIPMENT

Secateurs

Raffia

Stickpin

1. Prepare the materials by using secateurs to trim all dried stems to an even length of three to four inches. Remove any leaves or dried fragments from the lower half of each stem to ensure a neat, secure attachment.

2. Pick one star to be the center of the boutonniere; for example, the nigella, a berry stem, or a cluster of dried hydrangeas. Then use smaller and lighter elements to build around it, like Queen Anne's lace or grasses. Keep in mind that a boutonniere only has one face, so all the best flowers should be forward facing.

3. Tuck in feathers, curly twigs, or a small brooch for texture and personality.

4. Keep adding, adjusting, and playing with the tiny bouquet until you're happy with the shape. It should look balanced from the front, with a combination of thrill, chill, and spill (see page 17).

5. Using raffia, wrap the stems tightly several times one to two centimeters from the top of the stems. Then tie a small knot to secure the boutonniere.

6. Use a stickpin to secure the boutonniere to any ensemble, hat, or bag to add some everlasting elegance to any look du jour.

7. Store in a cool, dry place to preserve.

HOLIDAY AMBIANCE

IN FRANCE, THE TERM "HOLIDAY" refers to taking a vacation, unlike in America, where it's often associated specifically with winter festivities. These bouquets, however, capture the spirit of celebration—a "holiday ambiance" symbolizing universally significant occasions meant to bring people together. Every occasion presents an opportunity to create an atmosphere filled with the warmth, happiness, and celebration flowers provide, making each moment even more special.

Bouquet de Bonne Année

Happy New Year Bouquet

In France, wishing everyone a *bonne année* is a deeply ingrained tradition that is a way to express hope, joy, and prosperity for the year ahead. Interestingly, you have until the end of January to send or exchange these heartfelt wishes. This flower bouquet is a reflection of the new year, bursting with possibilities, freshness, and a subtle sparkle to bring joy into the home or hands of someone special. At L'Arrosoir, early January is one of our busiest periods, because gifting a bouquet is a timeless way in France to start the new year.

INGREDIENTS

3 chrysanthemums

3 stems acacia or other winter foliage

10 ranunculus

5 "Charlotte" ranunculus

3 pine branches

2 boulestriers (also known as balloon plant or hairy balls)

5 stems white waxflower

3 stems asparagus, sprayed with gold glitter

EQUIPMENT

Medium vase

Secateurs

1. Fill the vase two-thirds full with room-temperature water.
2. Remove any leaves that will fall below the waterline of the vase or interfere with the arrangement.
3. Begin building a spiral bouquet (see page 22): Hold a chrysanthemum stem in one hand. With the other hand, add an acacia stem or other foliage to create the base X shape. As you introduce new stems to form your spiral, cross each one diagonally over the previous one and rotate the bouquet slightly in the same direction with every addition.
4. Add the second chrysanthemum low in the bouquet; spin, and add the last chrysanthemum.
5. Add three ranunculus and give the bouquet a spin. Add two "Charlotte" ranunculus near each other, as if they are having a conversation on their own.
6. Add the remaining two acacia stems.
7. Continue building the bouquet by adding a pine branch, then spin the bouquet and position the second pine branch.
8. Add the remaining ranunculus in a second group; this gives a more natural look as if the ranunculus are growing together. I like to add the boulestriers near the end; this way, the green balls are peeking out on the side. Add the last pine branch, spin, and then place any remaining flower stems. Add the remaining "Charlotte" ranunculus strategically, so every flower is visible.
9. Incorporate the white waxflower stems, dispersing them throughout the bouquet.
10. Tuck in the sparkling asparagus stems so they are visible and sort of float over the bouquet. This is for a sparkly occasion, after all!
11. Secure the bouquet with raffia, wrapping it around the stems at least twice. Using the secateurs, trim the stems at an even angle, ensuring they will absorb water properly, then place the finished bouquet in the vase. Change the water daily to keep the flowers fresh and vibrant.

Fleurs pour la Saint-Valentin

Valentine's Day Flowers

Valentine's Day is always a special occasion at L'Arrosoir. It's my birthday, after all! So, naturally, we indulge in plenty of treats and champagne. But beyond the celebrations, we spend the day creating beautiful arrangements centered on the classic red rose. While some florists are moving away from red roses for Valentine's Day, I believe that when paired with other wildflowers and delicate winter foliage in a similar color scheme—and no white gypsophila *ever*—they take on an entirely new level of romance. With a line stretching out the door and around the block, these stunning bouquets fly off the shelves, bringing a great deal of Valentine's Day joy to some very lucky recipients. For this arrangement, I placed a simple cylinder vase inside a basket to contrast the elegant flowers and the natural charm of the basket.

INGREDIENTS

10 stems true blue eucalyptus

5 stems *Viburnum tinus* or other foliage

12 red roses (we like to use "Freedom" roses, which are a classic deep red rose)

10 anemones (also known as windflower)

7 tulips

5 butterfly ranunculus

EQUIPMENT

Medium vase

Raffia

Secateurs

1. Fill the vase three-quarters full with room-temperature water.

2. Remove the leaves from the lower part of the stems and the thorns from the roses.

3. Starting with a base of eucalyptus, begin building a spiral bouquet (see page 22): Hold the first stem in one hand. With the other hand, add a second eucalyptus stem to create a loose X shape. As you introduce new stems to form your spiral, cross each one diagonally over the previous one and rotate the bouquet slightly in the same direction with every addition.

4. Layer in a few stems of *Viburnum tinus*.

5. Add the red "Freedom" roses in small clusters of two or three, scattering them throughout. Next, incorporate the anemones, placing them between the roses.

6. Gently insert the tulips among the roses, letting their slender stems curve naturally. Continue layering *Viburnum tinus* to ensure foliage is spread throughout the bouquet.

7. Add the butterfly ranunculus, allowing them to weave in and around the other flowers. Their delicate beauty will give the bouquet a sweet, romantic feel.

8. Assess the arrangement, rotating it to check for balance. Add more eucalyptus or *Viburnum tinus* to fill gaps and make the bouquet full and lush.

9. Secure the bouquet by wrapping the stems tightly with raffia. Using the secateurs, trim all stems at an angle to the same length, ensuring that the bouquet stands tall and sits cleanly in the vase. Change the water daily to keep the flowers fresh and vibrant.

Table Printanière de l'Équinoxe

Spring Equinox Table

On the spring equinox, day and night are nearly equal in length, each lasting about twelve hours. The equinox has long been celebrated as a symbol of renewal, growth, and rebirth. It marks the return of longer days, warmer air, and the first signs of blooming flowers. When the light begins to overtake the dark, now that's something worth celebrating. We created this centerpiece as a tribute to this meaningful shift, the perfect focal point for a spring gathering.

INGREDIENTS

10 stems lisianthus

10 stems chamomile flower

10 hyacinth blooms

1 ivy vine

EQUIPMENT

Small transparent vase

Secateurs

1. Fill the vase halfway with room-temperature water.

2. Remove any leaves from the lower part of the stems.

3. Starting with a base of lisianthus, begin building a spiral bouquet (see page 22): Arrange a few lisianthus stems in an X shape. As you introduce new stems to form the spiral, cross each one diagonally over the previous one and rotate the bouquet slightly in the same direction with every addition.

4. Add chamomile to build structure and lightness.

5. Continue layering with hyacinth, rotating with each addition. Follow with more chamomile and lisianthus for a balanced mix of texture and color.

6. Vary the varieties and adjust the height of each stem to keep the bouquet visually interesting while maintaining a rounded shape.

7. Wrap the ivy vine tightly around the stems to secure the bouquet. Using the secateurs, trim all stems at an even angle to the same length, so the flowers rest just above the rim of the vase and softly spill over for a relaxed spring equinox celebration. Change the water daily to keep the flowers fresh and vibrant.

Muguet du Premier Mai

First of May Lily of the Valley

In France, May 1 is Fête du Travail, or Labor Day, but it's also a day filled with fun traditions. It marks the start of spring and is all about giving *le muguet*, or lily of the valley. The story goes that King Charles IX was so charmed by a gift of it on May 1 that he decided to give each lady in his court a bouquet of it every year. Now, on this day, the French offer lily of the valley to their loved ones as a symbol of good luck. At L'Arrosoir, we celebrate with pots of *muguet* to replant, as well as cut sprigs in bud vases. The scent of lily of the valley is sweet and delicate, and when paired with sweet peas and forget-me-nots, it's simply heavenly.

INGREDIENTS

15 stems *muguet* (lily of the valley)

6 stems sweet pea

9 stems *graminées* (wild grasses)

3 stems viburnum

EQUIPMENT

3 bud vases of mixed sizes and shapes

Couteau

1. Prepare the bud vases by filling each with room-temperature water (avoid adding water after the flowers are in place). Set the vases on the table beside the flowers.

2. Start by adding the *muguet* in mass, so that they really stand out. Using the couteau, trim each stem an even angle before adding to the vase.

3. Add two sweet peas in each vase, framing the *muguet*.

4. Add a few sprigs of *graminées* in each vase at varying heights.

5. Add a stem of viburnum as a finishing touch to these good luck charms. Change the water daily to keep the flowers fresh and vibrant.

Bouquet des Fiertés
Pride Rainbow Bouquet

Pride Week in Paris is radiant. The streets are lined with rainbow flags, and the massive parade down rue de Rivoli draws in millions of people from around the world. It's an outpouring of love, joy, and self expression. Every June, I create a rainbow bouquet just for fun and display it in the shop. I love playing with the full spectrum of color, but not necessarily in the classic rainbow order. Using chicken wire as a base inside the vessel gives the freedom to place each stem exactly where it feels right, letting the rainbow unfold organically and the colors beam with pride.

INGREDIENTS

3 branches tall foraged foliage
2 wild rose branches
10 large stems raspberry foliage
3 stems large green thistle
5 large yellow dahlias
7 large red dahlias
20 stems blue cornflower
15 stems purple aster
7 stems orange marigold
15 stems mililot (also known as yellow sweet clover)
3 stems blue delphinium

EQUIPMENT

Large urn or opaque container
Chicken wire
PVC floral tape
Couteau
Branch cutters

1. Fill the vase or container three-quarters full with room-temperature water.
2. Scrunch chicken wire into a ball, place it inside the vessel, and secure it with floral tape in a grid pattern to hold the stems in place.
3. Place all flowers on a clean surface separated by variety. Strip the lower leaves from all stems so they don't sit in water.
4. Give all stems a fresh diagonal cut using a couteau before adding them to the vessel. For thick branches, use branch cutters to cut the stems.
5. Build the foundation and shape using three tall foraged branches to define height and vertical movement. Next, add two wild rose branches, letting them arch outward.
6. Add the raspberry foliage stems to create a lush green framework, filling in the mid and lower areas.
7. Next, add the three thistle stems at different heights for sculptural accents.
8. Place five yellow dahlias at medium to high positions in a loose triangle.
9. Insert seven red dahlias slightly lower and deeper in the arrangement to add rich color and depth, and the red to the rainbow. Angle some dahlias to face different directions, as if the flowers are having a conversation.

10. Start to layer in the rest of the rainbow, adding the blue cornflowers in small groups.

11. Add the purple aster to create some volume, letting some poke out and spill over the sides of the arrangement.

12. Orange marigolds add the orange glow, and yellow melilot should dance around the bouquet, acting as an airy filler higher up in the bouquet.

13. Last but not least, use the blue delphiniums as vertical accents. Let some stems tower over the other flowers.

14. Take a step back and see if there are any stems that need adjusting. Spin the vessel a few times to check that the arrangement is well balanced. Change the water daily to keep the flowers fresh and vibrant.

Fleurs de la Fête Nationale

Bastille Day Blooms

I've always had a secret fondness for the French flag, possibly because it shares the same colors as the American flag I grew up with. Though blue, white, and red aren't shades I would naturally pair together in a bouquet, when blended in no particular color order, this arrangement becomes a patriotic centerpiece suited to celebrate Bastille Day and the Fourth of July. Each color stands out in its own way, representing different aspects of these celebrations. In Paris, much like my summers in the U.S., we spend the holiday outdoors with family. We devour the French version of hot dogs—spicy merguez sausages—and soak in the summer warmth as we wait for the fireworks to light up the night sky. The only difference? Here, the fireworks launch from behind the Eiffel Tower!

INGREDIENTS

2 prune branches
10 stems raspberry
3 tall blue delphiniums
1 blue hydrangea
1 white snow queen hydrangea
5 stems white achillea
5 stems Queen Anne's lace
5 stems white astilbe
5 to 7 red charm peonies
3 stems red lobelia
5 stems green thistle

EQUIPMENT

Vintage French jar (slightly narrow neck, round body)
Secateurs
Branch cutters

1. Prepare the vessel by filling it with room-temperature water.
2. Lay out all the flowers on a clean surface separated by variety.
3. Process the flowers by removing any leaves that would sit below the waterline.
4. Build the base structure by placing the two prune branches into the vintage jar, one tall and off-center for height and movement, and one angled to the side for asymmetry.
5. Add the raspberry stems around the lower area and sides, allowing some to spill over the edges of the jar.
6. Place the 3 tall blue delphiniums at different heights, mimicking the jets that blast over Paris on the 14th of July, one tallest and the two others just below.
7. Remember, hydrangeas need plenty of water, so gently plunge the hydrangea flower heads into water before adding them to the bouquet. Add the blue hydrangea near the bottom and slightly off center. Next, place the white snow queen hydrangea slightly behind the blue hydrangea, adding depth to the arrangement.
8. Scatter the five stems of white achillea, Queen Anne's lace, and white astilbe around the hydrangeas and delphiniums, pointing slightly outward like sparks and smoke.

Continues

9. Cluster the red charm peonies toward the front of the arrangement and add a few to the ten back as well, mimicking how peonies grow closely together in nature.

10. Add the three stems of red lobelia higher up among the delphiniums and prune branches to bring red color into the vertical space.

11. Place three stems of green thistle in the front of the arrangement and two in the back. These thistles are truly the fireworks in the arrangement!

12. Step back and make sure all the stems are visible.

13. The arrangement should feel natural and unrestrained. Adjust the stems as needed, letting the blue, white, and red tones flow together—like a family gathered on Bastille Day, watching fireworks light up the Parisian sky. Let it be wild, free, and full of life! Change the water daily to keep the flowers fresh and vibrant.

Fleurs de Gratitude
Thankful Flowers

Although Thanksgiving is not celebrated in France, I mark the occasion by hosting a dinner party for my expat friends. Because traditional ingredients are hard to find, we opt for a raclette dinner. Of course, fall flowers are an integral part of the celebration. The vibrant heart of the cabbage flower with its deep outer petals creates a rich contrast against dark red eucalyptus and bright orange berries, a perfect autumnal palette for late November. Tied with a trailing strand of ivy, the bouquet makes a statement, especially when displayed in a clear vase where the stems and foliage become part of the show. Cut extra short, it makes a beautiful Thanksgiving centerpiece.

INGREDIENTS

10 stems red eucalyptus

3 cabbage flowers

5 chrysanthemums

7 anemones (also known as windflower)

7 ranunculus

5 pink hellebores (also known as Christmas rose)

1 cotoneaster branch, cut into smaller pieces

5 scabiosa (also known as pincushion flower)

2 ivy vines

EQUIPMENT

Medium vase

Secateurs

1. Fill the vase two-thirds full with room-temperature water.

2. Prepare the flowers by removing the foliage from the bottom half of their stems, and then lay out the flowers by variety on a clean surface.

3. Begin building a spiral bouquet (see page 22): Hold one eucalyptus stem in one hand. With the other hand, add a second eucalyptus stem to form an X shape, placing it loosely to create an airy, structural base. Let the eucalyptus branches fan out gently. As you introduce new stems to form your spiral, cross each one diagonally over the previous one and rotate the bouquet slightly in the same direction with every addition.

4. Place the cabbage flowers off-center in the bouquet for an asymmetrical, relaxed look. Add each cabbage one at a time, then give the bouquet a gentle spin to check the balance and flow.

5. Add the chrysanthemums in a triangular shape around the cabbages. These will bring volume and texture to the bouquet.

6. Group the anemones together and place them in the bouquet two to three at a time; spin and add the remaining anemones.

7. Add a few more sprigs of eucalyptus, then place the ranunculus, spacing them around the other flowers.

8. Place three hellebores in the bouquet. Then, spin the bouquet and place the remaining two stems.

9. Incorporate the pieces of the cotoneaster branch, adding them throughout the bouquet. I like to spread

Continues

them around and always save a few for the end of the bouquet. Add the remaining anemones and spin, then the remaining ranunculus.

10. Add the scabiosa between the larger flowers. Their whimsical look will bring variation in height. Add the remaining eucalyptus and cotoneaster to complete the bouquet. Spin the bouquet one more time to make sure it looks even and adjust any flowers that need a little more movement.

11. Secure the bouquet with ivy vines for a unique variation. Using secateurs, trim all of the stems to an equal length, then place the flowers in the vase. Change the water daily to keep the flowers fresh and vibrant.

Bouquet Festif d'Hiver

Festive Winter Bouquet

There's something so wonderfully French about welcoming the holiday season with a bouquet of fresh flowers. During my first Noël at the shop, I was pleasantly overwhelmed by the fragrance of Christmas trees drifting down the streets of Paris. We sell hundreds of trees! In December, L'Arrosoir transforms into a winter garden overflowing with Christmas trees, red berries, holly, and moss-covered branches. Bringing seasonal nature indoors is L'Arrosoir's way of decking the halls. In this bouquet, I layered different varieties of pine and added a single-snipped poinsettia plant.

INGREDIENTS

6 pine branches

3 juniper branches

3 stems cyperus (also known as papyrus sedge or flatsedge)

3 stems ilex (also known as holly)

3 green thistles

5 stems waxflower

3 butterfly ranunculus

1 potted poinsettia

Small pine cones, glitter, or a sprig of mistletoe (optional)

EQUIPMENT

Medium vase

Branch cutters

Ribbon or twine

Secateurs

1. Fill the vase three-quarters full with cold water.

2. Using the branch cutters, trim the pine, juniper, and cyperus to workable lengths. Then snip the poinsettia flower as close to the root as possible so that you have a nice, long stem to work with. Remove any leaves from the lower part of the stems.

3. Starting with a base of pine, begin building a spiral bouquet (see page 22): Hold the first branch in one hand. With the other hand, add a second pine branch to create an X shape. As you introduce new stems to form your spiral, cross each one diagonally over the previous one and rotate the bouquet slightly in the same direction with every addition.

4. Layer in the juniper branches. Position them at an angle to create texture and movement within the bouquet. They have a slightly trailing nature, so let them extend out a bit from the central pine. Continue with the cyperus, rotating the bouquet and adding to create the spiral shape.

5. Add the ilex stems around the bouquet, either in the center or scattered evenly throughout the arrangement. The vibrant red berries will add a pop of color and holiday spirit to the design. Try to place them slightly off-center for a natural look.

6. Distribute the green thistles evenly, making sure to balance their spiky appearance with the more delicate flowers.

7. The waxflower is delicate and airy. Place it around the edges of the bouquet. It will fill in gaps and help give the arrangement a fuller, more textured appearance.

Continues

8. Add the butterfly ranunculus. These will flutter around the bouquet, adding a pretty and soft element to an otherwise very structured bouquet.

9. Place the snipped poinsettia branch into the center of the arrangement for a bold holiday focal point. Its vibrant red blooms will stand out against the greenery.

10. Wrap the bouquet with a festive ribbon or twine, and trim all of the stems evenly with secateurs before placing it in the vase. Feel free to add decorative elements like small pine cones, glitter, or even a sprig of mistletoe to make it extra special. Change the water daily to keep the flowers fresh and vibrant.

La Fin

Brocantes I Love

I'll never forget the first time I laid eyes on a *brocante*. I had just moved to Paris, and one happened to be unfolding right in front of Père Lachaise Cemetery, just steps from my new apartment. "What is this?!" I gasped to Ben, completely in awe. The streets were buzzing with energy, lined with quirky characters, hidden treasures, and little white tents where antiques dealers sipped wine while bargaining with Parisians. It was like stumbling into a scene from a movie. To me, brocanting is pure exhilaration. I chase them down whenever I have free time, and I'm still amazed by the finds and the prices! The very first thing I ever bought was a vintage map of Paris that day near Père Lachaise. Ten years later, it's hanging in Cove's bedroom.

BROCANTE DE LA BRUYÈRE—RUNGIS

170 avenue des Pépinières, 94550 Chevilly-Larue

Rungis, the Brocante de la Bruyère, located right next to the flower market, is my best-kept secret. Florence De Boisseau's selection of French antiques are so well displayed, you would think you were walking into a cinematic backdrop. Everything in this marvelous warehouse is for sale or rent, from set design to store props, home décor, and more. I had the joy of renting through Florence for my wedding in Montmartre, and together we transformed the museum into a vintage dream. She is so driven and a force! Every time I see her, she is simultaneously working on a million projects in her cabinet of curiosities. Florence has been a huge inspiration since I met her ten years ago. I am so delighted by her spirit whenever I have the chance to see her.

LADY M BROCANTE

@ladymbrocante

Because *brocantes* travel to different neighborhoods every weekend, I google *"brocantes* in Paris" to see the arrondissements where they are popping up. There are usually several going on in different neighborhoods at the same time. I love to check Lady M Brocante on Instagram and find out where her *brocante* will be, and because I love her stuff, I often follow her to wherever she is! Her stand is always perfectly curated, and a real *brocante* experience.

MARCHÉ AUX PUCES DE VANVES

16–18 avenue Georges Lafenestre, 75014 Paris

The reason I like Puces de Vanves is because of its consistency. I leave this *brocante*, which takes place every Saturday and Sunday in the 14th arrondissement, with at least one treasure every time. Rain or shine, these vendors are always set up and ready to sell their authentic goods. This is the particular *brocante* I use for sourcing flower frogs, which come in glass, metal, and porcelain. This *brocante* is hit or miss, but when it's a hit it can be exhilarating! I have found many decorations for my Parisian apartment here—even rugs, side tables, and stone garden pots. Come early, and don't forget to bring empty bags with you!

BELLE LURETTE

5 rue du Marché Popincourt, 75011 Paris

One day, on a walk from L'Arrosoir with my mom, we stopped at this large antiques store in the 11th arrondissement. We had to walk back to the shop, pick up the truck and drive back because we couldn't carry all the amazing mirrors, dressers, and knickknacks we purchased while shopping there. Since then, this has become one of my regular spots to stop by and pick up a new vase or two for L'Arrosoir, or chat with one of the knowledgeable antiques dealers.

L'OBJET QUI PARLE

86 rue des Martyrs, 75018 Paris

There are amazing shops all down the rue des Martyrs, and one of my favorites is this small, tucked-away *brocante*. The owner curates a fine selection of Parisian paintings and light fixtures. It is beautiful the way the shop glows from the street. Step into L'Objet qui Parle and be whisked back in time!

Glossary of French Floral Terms

blanc: white

Bonne Année: Happy New Year

bottes: bunches

Boule de Neige: snowball flower

boulestrier: balloon plant

brocante: flea market

champêtre: bucolic

chez toi: your place

coup de foudre: lightning strike (used to refer to love at first sight)

couteau: flower knife

emballage: wrapping

en libre service: self-service

éphémère: fleeting, not long-lasting

Fête du Travail: Labor Day

flâner: to move slowly, enjoying time and wandering aimlessly

flâneuse: aimless wanderer

fleurs bleues: someone romantic or sentimental

fleurettes: wildflowers

genêt: broom flower

graminées: grasses

jardin: garden

juste tulipes: just tulips

lumière d'été: summer light

mauvaises herbes: bad herbs (weeds)

muguet: lily of the valley

œillet: carnation

pensée: pansy

pique-fluers: flower frog

pour tout moment: for any time

sauvage: wild

secateurs: clippers or pruning shears

solifleur: bud vase

vert: green

Acknowledgments

Thank you to Christine and Alain, for hiring me on the spot and eventually selling me your beloved store.

Thank you to Leigh Eisenman, the best literary agent in the entire world. A chance seating arrangement at a friend's book event changed everything for me. Thank you for loving my story and helping me share it. Thank you for believing in L'Arrosoir and the power of flowers. I'm endlessly grateful for your texts, your motivation, and all the ways you've supported my family.

To Caitlin Leffel, Amanda Englander, Renée Bollier, Lisa Forde, Ivy McFadden, Kerry Acker, and everyone at Union Square & Co. who had a hand in bringing this book to life, thank you. From editing to design, your vision transformed notes scribbled on scrap paper into a tangible book.

I will always believe the most beautiful gift this book gave me was my friendship with the photographer, Katie Donnelly. Katie answers my calls on the first ring. She's the first to tell me my ideas aren't crazy—they're wonderful. Our babies bloomed together during the making of this book. I'll always treasure our photo shoots in Paris, savoring every moment. Thank you for your creativity, your strength, your light, and your gift. You're a cherished friend for the rest of *ma vie*.

Merci, Myra, for stepping in and saving the day, as you do best. Your precision, creativity, and perfectionism in bouquets were invaluable to the completion of this book. Your organization, your flair, and, yes, the caramel Frappuccinos, kept us going. Thank you so very much.

To Team L'Arrosoir in Paris, thank you for inspiring me every day with your talent and heart. Thank you for knowing exactly who I am, for letting me "tornado," and for standing beside me through every season. Thank you for letting me destroy the shop again and again for photos, parties, and wild ideas—and always putting it back together. A special thank-you to Renaud, the manager of L'Arrosoir Paris, who watches over the store as if it were his own so I can grow the business around the world. *Merci mille fois.*

To Debbie Spence, thank you for joining my team and helping edit this book. It truly takes a village, and I'm so grateful you're part of mine.

To my mom, Mary, my dad, Mark, and my sister, Laurel, thank you for loving me through every phase and supporting me, even with an ocean between us. My dad helped me move to Paris, and my mom has more French stamps in her passport than most, from visiting so often. I'm beyond lucky to have you. Your love of flowers and horticulture runs in my roots—I can only hope the same will happen for Cove. Now that I'm a parent, I can only imagine how it felt when I chose to move so far away. Thank you for supporting my ambition and for raising me to be confident in my choices.

Paris gave me Anna, and for that I'll always be *reconnaissante*. Anna, thank you for being my soulmate in this city. Because of you I see endless possibilities. Thank you for answering all my book questions, Paris questions, travel questions, my annoying questions. Thank you for your support and for letting us barge into your apartment with flowers and cameras. I'm sorry I always get dirt everywhere—thank you for cleaning it up. Thank you for being you.

To Emily, Dagny Dis, Ajiri, Chloé, and all the friends Paris brought into my life. Thank you for always supporting me and always supporting L'Arrosoir. And Pearl—thank you for nourishing me (and Cove!) during my pregnancy and the writing of this book at my favorite neighborhood spot, The Hood. Your care and kindness are a part of this story too.

The Empty Vase in West Hollywood is where I first realized that working in a flower shop was my actual dream job. I only worked there for three months before deciding to move to Paris, but those months changed me. Not only did the team encourage me to go, they even wrote a letter to the French embassy to support my visa application. Saeed, you continue to be a huge inspiration to me. I admire the way you run your business—with boldness, bravery, and massive guts!

Thank you to Ben's family for welcoming a twenty-two-year-old Californian who didn't speak a word of French with open arms. You embraced me even more because of our cultural differences. I know how rare that is, and I'll never take it for granted. I truly hit the jackpot. Your love and support, especially throughout this project, has meant the world. When I had photo shoots or deadlines with a newborn baby, Ben's mom Isabelle or stepmom Geraldine would fly in from Nice just to help. I truly couldn't have done this without you.

Florence de Boissieu—my vintage queen! You amazed me from the first time I saw you in action at Rungis. Your enthusiasm, your passion—they're electric. Thank you for letting me shoot in your stunning store, and for continuing to be such a loyal friend and an incredible asset to L'Arrosoir in both Paris and Oslo.

To my beloved vendors at Rungis, rain or shine, you're there at 3 a.m. with the freshest stems and the warmest smiles. You are my cherished colleagues and a constant source of inspiration. Thank you for your dedication to the craft, and for filling this book with the most beautiful French flowers imaginable.

To my incredible team at L'Arrosoir Oslo, thank you for diving into this Parisian adventure in Norway. I've learned so much from you, and I'm honored to work alongside your passion, drive, and artistry every single day. Thank you for allowing me to be everywhere at once and for executing the vision with so much heart.

Sandra Sigman, when you first walked into my store with your beaming smile and kind presence, I just knew I'd met someone special. Thank you for being so generous with your wisdom, whether about business, life, or flowers. You are an incredible force, and someone I truly admire. So many people look up to you, including me.

Félicie, thank you for your social media magic and your thoughtful insights across every project. Your support behind the scenes has been so valuable.

To my best friends from home—you know who you are. Thank you for pushing me to chase my French crush and take the leap to Paris. Thank you for always reminding me who I am and where I come from. Thank you for never forgetting me, for showing up, and for traveling across the world to visit. I fell in love with Paris by sharing it with you. You've been there for me my whole life, and I'm endlessly grateful.

And Benjamin . . . thank you for giving me Paris. None of this would have happened without you. I remember when we met, I thought, *whoever marries this man will be the luckiest person in the world.* I still can't believe I'm that lucky wife. I couldn't have dreamed up anything more. Thank you for being there on every call, every meeting, and for holding me steady when I'm spiraling and cheering me on when I'm shining. I'll never forget when my computer crashed mid-book and you jumped in and fixed everything, because that's what you do. You always fix everything. Being with you anywhere is my happy place. And *surtout*, thank you for giving me Cove. *Je t'aime beaucoup.*

ACKNOWLEDGMENTS • 215

Index

NOTE: Page references in *italics* refer to photos.

A

All-Mimosa Bouquet (Bouquet Tout Mimosa), *82,* 83
ambiance, about, 10, 11, 13, 14–15, 22. *See also* everlasting ambiance; holiday ambiance; impressionist-inspired ambiance; indoor garden ambiance; L'Arrosoir ambiance bouquets; minimalist ambiance; Parisian ambiance; romantic ambiance
anemones
    Ballerinas in Bloom Bouquet (Bouquet Ballerines en Fleurs), 113–114, *115*
    Flowers of the Flea Market (Les Fleurs de la Brocante), 84–86, *85*
    Parisian Signature Bouquet (Bouquet Signature Parisien), *76,* 77–78, *79*
    Shades of Amethyst (Nuances d'Améthyste), *144,* 145–146, *147*
    Still Life with Anemones (Nature Morte aux Anémones), *116,* 117
    Thankful Flowers (Fleurs de Gratitude), 200–202, *201*
    Valentine's Day Flowers (Fleurs pour la Saint-Valentin), 184, *185*

B

Ballerinas in Bloom Bouquet (Bouquet Ballerines en Fleurs), 113–114, *115*
Bastille Day Blooms (Fleurs de la Fête Nationale), *196,* 197–198, *199*
Being Blue Flowers Bouquet (Être Fleurs Bleues), *48, 66,* 67–68, *69*
Belle Lurette (brocante/flea market), 208
Blanc et Vert (White and Green), 32–34, *33*

Bocaux d'Herbier (Herbarium Jars), 131, *132–133*
Bocaux Magiques (Magic Jars), *162–163,* 170, *171*
Bouquet Ballerines en Fleurs (Ballerinas in Bloom Bouquet), 113–114, *115*
Bouquet Champêtre (Wildflower Bouquet), *46,* 47
Bouquet Coup de Coeur (Bouquet for Your Crush), *60,* 61
Bouquet de Bonne Année (Happy New Year Bouquet), *182,* 183
Bouquet de Fines Herbes de Cuisine (Kitchen Herb Bouquet), 136, *137*
Bouquet de Fritillaires Plein de Fantaisie (Playful Fritillaria Bouquet), 160, *161*
Bouquet de Roses d'Espérance (Hope Roses Bouquet), 53–54, *55*
Bouquet des Fiertés (Pride Rainbow Bouquet), *192–193,* 194–195
Bouquet Festif d'Hiver (Festive Winter Bouquet), 203–205, *204*
Bouquet Fleurettes (Small Flowers Bouquet), *90,* 91
Bouquet for Your BFF (Un Bouquet pour Ton Meilleur Ami(e)), *148–149,* 150
Bouquet for Your Crush (Bouquet Coup de Coeur), *60,* 61
Bouquet Frais aux Notes d'Agrumes (Fresh Citrus Bouquet), *134,* 135
Bouquet Lumière d'Été (Summer Light Bouquet), *44,* 45
Bouquet Signature du Jardin d'Intérieur (Indoor Garden Signature Bouquet), *120,* 121–122, *122*
Bouquet Signature Éternel (Everlasting Signature Bouquet), 164–165, *165, 166–167*
Bouquet Signature Impressionniste (Impressionist Signature Bouquet), *98,* 99–100, *101*

Bouquet Signature Parisien (Parisian Signature Bouquet), 76, *77–78*, *79*
Bouquet Signature Romantique (Romantic Signature Bouquet), *50*, 51–52, *52*
Bouquet Tout Mimosa (All-Mimosa Bouquet), *82*, 83
Boutonnière Séchée (Dried Boutoniere), *178*, 179
brocantes (flea markets), 18, 207–208
Bud Vases of L'Arrosoir (Soliflor de L'Arrosoir), *42*, *43*

C

Candélabre Décoratif (Embellished Candelabra), 70–73, *71*, *72*
champêtre style, 10, 27, 28, 46
Charcuterie Board, Curated (Plateau de Charcuterie Raffiné), 35–37, *36*
Cheminée Parisienne (Parisian Mantle Arrangement), 87–88, *89*
Citrus Bouquet, Fresh (Bouquet Frais aux Notes d'Agrumes), *134*, 135
Classic French Style (Style Classique Français), *156*, 157–158, *159*
color scheme, about, 14–15, 32
cosmos
    Classic French Style (Style Classique Français), *156*, 157–158, *159*
    Cosmo Fields Forever (Cosmo pour Toujours), *38*, 39–40, *41*
    Small Flowers Bouquet (Bouquet Fleurettes), *90*, 91
    Wildflower Bouquet (Bouquet Champêtre), 46, *47*
Couronne à Tout Occasion (Wreath for All Occasions), *172*, 173
craft paper, wrapping bouquets with, 17
Curated Charcuterie Board (Plateau de Charcuterie Raffiné), 35–37, *36*
cut flowers, daily care of, 14, 25

D

daffodils
    Daffodil Ensemble (Ensemble de Jonquilles), 154, *155*
    Impressionist Signature Bouquet (Bouquet Signature Impressionniste), *98*, 99–100, *101*
daily care of cut flowers, 14, 25
delphinium
    Being Blue Flowers Bouquet (Être Fleurs Bleues), *48*, *66*, 67–68, *69*
    Cosmo Fields Forever (Cosmo pour Toujours), *38*, 39–40, *41*
    Delphinium Dream (Rêve de Delphinium), 151, *152–153*
    Eternal Garden (Jardin Éternel), *174–175*, 176, *177*
    Monet's Garden (Le Jardin de Monet), *110*, 111–112
    The Secret Garden (Le Jardin Secret), *128–129*, 130
Dried Boutoniere (Boutonnière Séchée), *178*, 179
dried flowers. *See* everlasting ambiance

E

Embellished Candelabra (Candélabre Décoratif), 70–73, *71*, *72*
Enchanted Garden Table (La Table du Jardin Enchanté), *57*, 58–59, *59*
Ensemble de Jonquilles (Daffodil Ensemble), 154, *155*
equipment for flower arranging, 18, *19*
Eternal Garden (Jardin Éternel), *174–175*, 176, *177*
Être Fleurs Bleues (Being Blue Flowers Bouquet), *48*, *66*, 67–68, *69*
everlasting ambiance, 163–179
    about, 163
    Dried Boutoniere (Boutonnière Séchée), *178*, 179
    Eternal Garden (Jardin Éternel), *174–175*, 176, *177*
    Everlasting Signature Bouquet (Bouquet Signature Éternel), 164–165, *165*, *166–167*
    Magic Jars (Bocaux Magiques), *162–163*, 170, *171*
    Preserving Petals (Préserver les Pétales), *168*, 169
    Wreath for All Occasions (Couronne à Tout Occasion), *172*, 173

F

Festive Winter Bouquet (Bouquet Festif d'Hiver), 203–205, *204*
First of May Lily of the Valley (Muguet du Premier Mai), 190, *191*
Flea Market, Flowers of the (Les Fleurs de la Brocante), 84–86, *85*
flea markets (brocantes), 18, 207–208
Fleurs de Gratitude (Thankful Flowers), 200–202, *201*
Fleurs de la Fête Nationale (Bastille Day Blooms), *196*, 197–198, *199*
Fleurs pour Anna Wintour (Flowers for Anna Wintour), 80, *81*
Fleurs pour la Saint-Valentin (Valentine's Day Flowers), 184, *185*
flower arranging
    ambiance for, 10, 11, 13, 14–15, 22
    champêtre style for, 10, 27, 28, 46
    color scheme for, 14–15, 32
    daily care of cut flowers, 14, 25
    equipment and tools for, 18, *19*
    floral frogs for, 18, 121–122, *122*
    flower markets as source of flowers, 14, 15
    flower selection for, 15
    French floral terms glossary, 210
    French lifestyle and, 13
    French spiral bouquet for, 14, 22–25, *23*, *24*
    by L'Arrosoir (flower shop), 9–11, *10*, 13, 14–15, *17*
    securing bouquets, 17, 22, 25
    thrill, chill, spill for, 17
    vases and vessels for, *20*, 21
    wrapping bouquets, 17
flower knife (couteau), 14, 18
Flowers for Anna Wintour (Fleurs pour Anna Wintour), 80, *81*
Flowers of the Flea Market (Les Fleurs de la Brocante), 84–86, *85*
foliage, stripping, 22
food, Curated Charcuterie Board (Plateau de Charcuterie Raffiné), 35–37, *36*
foraging, about, 10

French floral terms glossary, 210
French spiral bouquet, about, 14, 22–25, *23*, *24*. See also flower arranging
French Style, Classic (Style Classique Français), *156*, 157–158, *159*
fritillaria
    Impressionist Signature Bouquet (Bouquet Signature Impressionniste), *98*, 99–100, *101*
    Petite Table Centerpieces (Petits Centres de Table), *92*, *93*, *94*, *95*
    Playful Fritillaria Bouquet (Bouquet de Fritillaires Plein de Fantaisie), 160, *161*
    Van Gogh's Fritillaria (Les Fritillaires de Van Gogh), *106*, 107, *108*, *109*

G

glossary, French floral terms, 210

H

Happy New Year Bouquet (Bouquet de Bonne Année), *182*, 183
Herbarium Jars (Bocaux d'Herbier), 131, *132–133*
Herb Bouquet, Kitchen (Bouquet de Fines Herbes de Cuisine), 136, *137*
holiday ambiance, 181–205
    about, 181
    Bastille Day Blooms (Fleurs de la Fête Nationale), *196*, 197–198, *199*
    Festive Winter Bouquet (Bouquet Festif d'Hiver), 203–205, *204*
    First of May Lily of the Valley (Muguet du Premier Mai), 190, *191*
    Happy New Year Bouquet (Bouquet de Bonne Année), *182*, 183
    Pride Rainbow Bouquet (Bouquet des Fiertés), *192–193*, 194–195
    Spring Equinox Table (Table Printanière de l'Équinoxe), *186*, *187*, *188*, *189*

holiday ambiance *(continued)*
  Thankful Flowers (Fleurs de Gratitude), 200–202, *201*
  Valentine's Day Flowers (Fleurs pour la Saint-Valentin), 184, *185*
  Hope Roses Bouquet (Bouquet de Roses d'Espérance), 53–54, *55*

I

impressionist-inspired ambiance, 97–117
  about, 97
  Ballerinas in Bloom Bouquet (Bouquet Ballerines en Fleurs), 113–114, *115*
  Impressionist Signature Bouquet (Bouquet Signature Impressionniste), *98*, 99–100, *101*
  Monet's Garden (Le Jardin de Monet), *110*, 111–112
  Renoir's Garden (Inspiré du Jardin de Renoir), *102–103*, 104–105, *105*
  Still Life with Anemones (Nature Morte aux Anémones), *116*, 117
  Van Gogh's Fritillaria (Les Fritillaires de Van Gogh), *106*, 107, *108*, *109*
indoor garden ambiance, 119–137
  about, 119
  Fresh Citrus Bouquet (Bouquet Frais aux Notes d'Agrumes), 134, *135*
  Herbarium Jars (Bocaux d'Herbier), 131, *132–133*
  Indoor Garden Signature Bouquet (Bouquet Signature du Jardin d'Intérieur), *120*, 121–122, *122*
  Kitchen Herb Bouquet (Bouquet de Fines Herbes de Cuisine), 136, *137*
  Little Indoor Garden (Petit Jardin d'Interieur), 126, *127*
  The Secret Garden (Le Jardin Secret), *128–129*, 130
  Untamed Bouquet (Le Bouquet Sauvage), 123–125, *124*
Inspiré du Jardin de Renoir (Renoir's Garden), *102–103*, 104–105, *105*
ivy, about, 22

J

Jardin Éternel (Eternal Garden), *174–175*, 176, *177*
Just Tulips (Juste Tulipes), 142, *143*

K

Kitchen Herb Bouquet (Bouquet de Fines Herbes de Cuisine), 136, *137*

L

Lady M Brocante (brocante/flea market), 207–208
L'Arrosoir ambiance bouquets, 27–47
  about, 27
  Bud Vases of L'Arrosoir (Soliflor de L'Arrosoir), 42, *43*
  Cosmo Fields Forever (Cosmo pour Toujours), *38*, 39–40, *41*
  Curated Charcuterie Board (Plateau de Charcuterie Raffiné), 35–37, *36*
  L'Arrosoir Signature Bouquet (Le Bouquet Signature de L'Arrosoir), 28–29, *29*, 30–31
  Summer Light Bouquet (Bouquet Lumière d'Été), 44, *45*
  White and Green (Blanc et Vert), 32–34, *33*
  Wildflower Bouquet (Bouquet Champêtre), 46, *47*
L'Arrosoir (flower shop), 9–11, *10*, 13, *14–15*, 17
La Table du Jardin Enchanté (Enchanted Garden Table), *57*, 58–59, *59*
Le Bouquet Sauvage (Untamed Bouquet), 123–125, *124*
Le Bouquet Signature de L'Arrosoir (L'Arrosoir Signature Bouquet), 28–29, *29*, 30–31
Le Jardin de Monet (Monet's Garden), *110*, 111–112
Le Jardin Secret (The Secret Garden), *128–129*, 130
Les Fleurs de la Brocante (Flowers of the Flea Market), 84–86, *85*
Lily of the Valley, First of May (Muguet du Premier Mai), 190, *191*

Little Indoor Garden (Petit Jardin d'Interieur), 126, *127*
L'Objet qui Parle (brocante/flea market), 208

M

Magic Jars (Bocaux Magiques), *162–163, 170, 171*
Marché aux Puces de Vanves (brocante/flea market), 208
minimalist ambiance, 139–161
    about, 139
    Bouquet for Your BFF (Un Bouquet pour Ton Meilleur Ami(e)), *148–149,* 150
    Classic French Style (Style Classique Français), *156,* 157–158, *159*
    Daffodil Ensemble (Ensemble de Jonquilles), 154, *155*
    Delphinium Dream (Rêve de Delphinium), 151, *152–153*
    Just Tulips (Juste Tulipes), 142, *143*
    Playful Fritillaria Bouquet (Bouquet de Fritillaires Plein de Fantaisie), 160, *161*
    Shades of Amethyst (Nuances d'Améthyste), *144,* 145–146, *147*
    Small Passion Garden (Petit Jardin de Passion), *140,* 141
mirrors, for display, 25
Monet's Garden (Le Jardin de Monet), *110,* 111–112
Muguet du Premier Mai (First of May Lily of the Valley), 190, *191*
music, for flowers, 25

N

Nature Morte aux Anémones (Still Life with Anemones), *116,* 117
Nuances d'Améthyste (Shades of Amethyst), *144,* 145–146, *147*

P

paper, wrapping bouquets with, 17
Parfum d'Amour (Scent of Love), *62–63,* 64, *65*
Parisian ambiance, 75–95
    All-Mimosa Bouquet (Bouquet Tout Mimosa), *82,* 83
    Flowers for Anna Wintour (Fleurs pour Anna Wintour), 80, *81*
    Flowers of the Flea Market (Les Fleurs de la Brocante), 84–86, *85*
    Parisian Mantle Arrangement (Cheminée Parisienne), 87–88, *89*
    Parisian Signature Bouquet (Bouquet Signature Parisien), *76,* 77–78, *79*
    Petite Table Centerpieces (Petits Centres de Table), 92, *93, 94, 95*
    Small Flowers Bouquet (Bouquet Fleurettes), *90,* 91
Petit Jardin de Passion (Small Passion Garden), *140,* 141
Petit Jardin d'Interieur (Little Indoor Garden), 126, *127*
Petits Centres de Table (Petite Table Centerpieces), 92, *93, 94, 95*
Plateau de Charcuterie Raffiné (Curated Charcuterie Board), 35–37, *36*
Playful Fritillaria Bouquet (Bouquet de Fritillaires Plein de Fantaisie), 160, *161*
Preserving Petals (Préserver les Pétales), *168,* 169
Pride Rainbow Bouquet (Bouquet des Fiertés), *192–193,* 194–195
pruning shears (secateurs), 15, 18, 25
Puces de Vanves (brocante/flea market), 208

R

raffia, securing bouquets with, 17, 22, 25
Renoir's Garden (Inspiré du Jardin de Renoir), *102–103, 104–105,* 105
Rêve de Delphinium (Delphinium Dream), 151, *152–153*

romantic ambiance, 49–73
    about, 49
    Being Blue Flowers Bouquet (Être Fleurs Bleues), *48*, *66*, *67*–*68*, *69*
    Bouquet for Your Crush (Bouquet Coup de Coeur), *60*, 61
    Embellished Candelabra (Candélabre Décoratif), 70–73, *71*, *72*
    Enchanted Garden Table (La Table du Jardin Enchanté), *57*, 58–59, *59*
    Hope Roses Bouquet (Bouquet de Roses d'Espérance), 53–54, *55*
    Romantic Signature Bouquet (Bouquet Signature Romantique), *50*, 51–52, *52*
    Scent of Love (Parfum d'Amour), *62*–*63*, 64, *65*
roses
    Fresh Citrus Bouquet (Bouquet Frais aux Notes d'Agrumes), *134*, 135
    Hope Roses Bouquet (Bouquet de Roses d'Espérance), 53–54, *55*
    Indoor Garden Signature Bouquet (Bouquet Signature du Jardin d'Intérieur), *120*, 121–122, *122*
    Pride Rainbow Bouquet (Bouquet des Fiertés), *192*–*193*, 194–195
    Romantic Signature Bouquet (Bouquet Signature Romantique), *50*, 51–52, *52*
    Valentine's Day Flowers (Fleurs pour la Saint-Valentin), *184*, *185*
Rungis (Brocante de la Bruyère market), 14, 15, 207

S

Scent of Love (Parfum d'Amour), *62*–*63*, 64, *65*
secateurs (pruning shears), 15, 18, 25
The Secret Garden (Le Jardin Secret), *128*–*129*, 130
Shades of Amethyst (Nuances d'Améthyste), *144*, 145–146, *147*
signature bouquets
    Everlasting Signature Bouquet (Bouquet Signature Éternel), 164–165, *165*, 166–167
    Impressionist Signature Bouquet (Bouquet Signature Impressionniste), *98*, 99–100, *101*
    Indoor Garden Signature Bouquet (Bouquet Signature du Jardin d'Intérieur), *120*, 121–122, *122*
    L'Arrosoir Signature Bouquet (Le Bouquet Signature de L'Arrosoir), 28–29, *29*, 30–31
    Parisian Signature Bouquet (Bouquet Signature Parisien), *76*, 77–78, *79*
    Romantic Signature Bouquet (Bouquet Signature Romantique), *50*, 51–52, *52*
Small Flowers Bouquet (Bouquet Fleurettes), *90*, 91
Small Passion Garden (Petit Jardin de Passion), *140*, 141
Soliflor de L'Arrosoir (Bud Vases of L'Arrosoir), 42, *43*
spiral bouquet design, about, 14, 22–25, *23*, *24*
Spring Equinox Table (Table Printanière de l'Équinoxe), *186*, 187, *188*, 189
stems, cleaning, 22
Still Life with Anemones (Nature Morte aux Anémones), *116*, 117
Style Classique Français (Classic French Style), *156*, 157–158, *159*
Summer Light Bouquet (Bouquet Lumière d'Été), 44, 45

T

Table Printanière de l'Équinoxe (Spring Equinox Table), *186*, 187, *188*, 189
Thankful Flowers (Fleurs de Gratitude), 200–202, *201*
thrill, chill, spill, 17
tulips
    Just Tulips (Juste Tulipes), 142, *143*
    The Secret Garden (Le Jardin Secret), *128*–*129*, 130
    Valentine's Day Flowers (Fleurs pour la Saint-Valentin), *184*, *185*

U

Un Bouquet pour Ton Meilleur Ami(e) (Bouquet for Your BFF), *148–149*, 150
Untamed Bouquet (Le Bouquet Sauvage), 123–125, *124*

V

Valentine's Day Flowers (Fleurs pour la Saint-Valentin), 184, *185*
Van Gogh's Fritillaria (Les Fritillaires de Van Gogh), *106*, 107, *108*, *109*
vases and vessels, *20*, 21

W

White and Green (Blanc et Vert), 32–34, *33*
Wildflower Bouquet (Bouquet Champêtre), 46, *47*
Winter Bouquet, Festive (Bouquet Festif d'Hiver), 203–205, *204*
wrapping of bouquets, 17
Wreath for All Occasions (Couronne à Tout Occasion), *172*, 173